LONGMAN IMPRINT BOOK

Introducing
....

Newspapers, advertising, television, radio and film

Selected and edited by Peter Griffiths

General editor: Michael Marland
Series consultant: Geoff Barton

Peter Griffiths worked in Education for 17 years, as an
English teacher and lecturer and as co-warden of the ILEA
English Centre. Then he moved into Educational Television.
For 11 years he was series producer of the award-winning
ITV/C4 series *The English Programme*, specialising in
resources for English and Media Studies teaching in the
upper forms of secondary schools. He produced the only
educational programme to be awarded an International
Emmy and, in 1994, was given the Royal Television Society's
Education Award for his programme comparing the book
and the film of *My Left Foot*.

Longman Imprint Books

General Editor: Michael Marland

New Titles

Previously published titles

Contents

CONTENTS

The National Curriculum

The National Curriculum for English says that pupils should read

'a wide range of media, *e.g. magazines, newspapers, radio, television, film.* They should be given opportunities to analyse and evaluate such material, which should be of high quality and represent a range of forms and purposes, and different structural and presentational devices.'

This collection contains texts taken from each of the media mentioned above. In each section there is a variety of texts. Each is a good example of its particular form, or genre – whether it be an editorial from a newspaper, an advertising poster, a comedy exploiting the medium of radio, an extract from a television soap opera or a classic film.

These texts were created in many different forms and for many different purposes: to inform, persuade, amuse, shock, thrill, and so on. As a result, reading them and then discussing and writing about them, develops our ideas and feelings, our moral and emotional understanding. There is a wide range of presentational devices – news items, photos, scripts, letters, eye-witness reports, etc.

The book also contains a variety of study activities designed to increase readers' understanding and critical awareness, through analysis, evaluation, and comparison of texts and by looking at their social and historical contexts.

Comparing texts from different media

Tragedy: World Press Photos/It was the Christians/Murderers, torturers, rapists

Humour: Hancock's Half-Hour/Word of Mouth/ Monty Python/Absolutely Fabulous

Environment: And you thought twisters only hit America/ Bradwell Nature Trail

Health: Anorexic models/Ads/Jimmy's/Casualty

Women: Anorexic models/World Press Photo 1993/ Web of fear!/Absolutely Fabulous/The Third Man

Men: World Press Photo 1992/Oasis/Hancock's Half-Hour/ Word of Mouth/Raiders of the Lost Ark/The Third Man

Race: World Press Photo 1993/S-Curl ad/Word of Mouth/ Raiders of the Lost Ark

Children and Young People: Jane Eyre/Brookside/ Absolutely Fabulous

Heroes and villains: Oasis/Jane Eyre/Raiders of the Lost Ark/ The Third Man

Skills and activities

Speaking and Listening: talking in pairs, discussing in groups, reporting to the class, making a speech, hotseating, roleplay, tape-recording, performing.

Writing: news items for newspapers and radio, letters to a newspaper/magazine/organisation, reviews, stories, lists, project reports, summarising, translating into another medium, diary, radio play, voice-over, film and television scripts for various genres (e.g. comedy sketch, documentary, soap, adventure film).

Media: laying out a front page, designing an advert, preparing a storyboard, recording a radio play, creating a PR pamphlet, set designing, developing a comedy act, taking and analysing photos.

Introduction

This book contains scripts that are funny, tragic, shocking, silly, thought-provoking, outrageous. They are taken from many media – newspapers, magazines, adverts, radio, film and television. Some are eye-witness reports of actual happenings; others are fictions – some realistic, some fantastic, some a mixture.

They all come from larger works – a whole newspaper, for instance – or were written in order to be transformed into another medium – a television programme, for example. Nearly all involved words alongside pictures. The film scripts are obvious examples there, and they ended up in the form of moving pictures accompanied by a mix of spoken dialogue, music and other sounds.

Most of the pieces, and especially the radio, television and film scripts, benefit from being read aloud. If you are reading in a group, it will help if you choose one person to be the author: to read introductions, stage directions, etc.

You can read them just as you'd read a short story or a playscript – as though they were meant to be words by themselves on a page. So you'll take note of the storyline, 'characters', setting, and the ways the author uses language to create moods and feelings and to raise ideas. And you'll ask yourself such questions as: what viewpoint is the author taking to the events described? who am I being asked to admire? who to despise?

But you'll get more out of the reading the more you try to recreate in your head the actual work on the newspaper page or on the radio or in the cinema. Then you'll also take into account each different medium's way of conveying ideas and feelings: how it uses headlines (news-papers) or just sounds (radio) or a combination of pictures and sounds (film and television) to encourage us to think in a certain way about what it is depicting.

Looking closely at the illustrations in this book can help you with that sometimes.

You can also get more out of your reading by visualising the scenes. For television and film scripts you'll need to work out what the 'characters', whether real people or fictional creations, would look like, where they would be placed in the picture, how they would move about, how the camera might move to follow them or to look at something else in the scene.

You'll also get more enjoyment, and understand the pieces better, if you connect them to media works that you know already. You can consider how different groups of people are represented – in the texts here and in other media texts you come across. For instance, you might compare the women behaving badly in the extract from *Absolutely Fabulous* with any examples you know of men behaving badly.

As well as comparing by subject-matter or theme, you can compare across a genre. For example, what do the examples of television sitcoms have in common? How do they differ? Why do you think that is?

The main thing to remember is that you already have masses of experience of the media. The more you draw on that experience, the more you'll develop your enjoyment and understanding of these pieces, too.

Peter Griffiths

Newspapers and magazines

The British read more newspapers per head than any other nation. And not just for news. Papers contain a lot of the ingredients of magazines and some even include a whole magazine at least once a week. With some it's a matter of opinion whether they deserve the title *news*paper at all. In this chapter it is sometimes easy to recognise that an item comes from a newspaper; sometimes it's not.

A famous newspaper editor, C. P. Scott, once said: 'Comment is free but facts are sacred.' But you can't separate facts and opinion so easily. The 'facts' you think worth collecting, the things you leave out and the way that you present them – all these help to indicate your opinion. So, every item in a newspaper or magazine carries a point of view.

The front page of a paper or magazine says: look at this; it's so important for our readers that they will buy the paper; this is the way the world is; this is good (or bad); these people are heroes (or villains) to be admired (or not). The headline says: look at this; it's important; here's a summary of the story; here's our attitude (for/against/matter-of-fact/cool/sensational etc.).

Ad chief gives Vogue a lean time

by ANNIE LEASK

FASHION magazine Vogue has been hit by a costly advertising ban for using "skeleton-thin" models in its latest issue.

The Omega watch company has withdrawn its campaign because of the pictures of women modelling underwear in the June edition.

Omega boss Giles Rees said he was appalled by the photos.

"I thought it was irresponsible for a leading magazine, which should be setting an example, to select models of anorexic proportions," said Mr Rees.

He thought the article "made every effort to accentuate their skeletal appearance".

He added: "Since Vogue presumably targets an audience which includes young and impressionable females, its creators must surely be aware that they will inevitably be influenced by what laughably passes for fashion in these pages."

Mr Rees was unable to put a figure on the amount of money involved. He said Omega used models such as Cindy Crawford and Elle MacPherson for their watch campaigns but, although they were slim, they were not excessively thin.

Dr Dee Dawson, who runs anorexia clinic Rhodes Farm, backed Mr Rees. Last month one of her patients was approached by two model agencies.

She said one of the models was clearly ill. "You cannot look like that unless you are sick — it is just impossible.

"I could not believe that Vogue could use pictures like that after all the recent publicity about the use of models with anorexia. These magazines do affect the way girls and women think of themselves."

Last night a spokesman for Vogue claimed that Mr Rees had complained about a feature on watches and had then extended his protest to include the fashion pictures.

The spokesman denied magazines such as Vogue had any influence on girls becoming anorexic. "We only use models who are healthy and well," he insisted. "The idea that we promote anorexia is preposterous[1]."

---

[1] **preposterous** – ridiculous

EDITORIAL

Let there be flesh

GIRLS of 10 and upwards who are watching their weight with an eye to the catwalk should relax, and be encouraged to take a second helping of plum duff. Venus de Milo[2] is back in fashion, and a sudden question mark has appeared over the heads of skinny models, first made fashionable by Twiggy of bygone days.

Vogue magazine, with which all who go to the right sort of dentist will be familiar, has had a shock. It has been printing pictures of skinny girls on whom fashionable clothes hang seductively. Omega, the Swiss watch company, threatened to withdraw its advertising (although it retreated from doing so) in protest against such pictures, which it described as "incredibly irresponsible". Beyond this protest is Omega's distaste for advertising that will strongly appeal to young impressionable girls, and may encourage them to slim to the point of anorexia.

In our book, advertisers should not set about trying to influence editorial content. In this circumstance, though, there are extenuating circumstances. A fashion cult which persuades young girls to worry about their weight and so encourages some of them to starve themselves is undesirable. Furthermore, on the edge of this controversy are pictures which have appeared elsewhere of very young girls who may attract paedophiles.

There is a tendency for the fashion industry to behave as lord of all it portrays. No great harm is done by advising it that there are limits to the art of persuading women to invest in the unattainable. A skeletal model on the catwalk promotes not clothes but fantasy. There will be mumbles from the fashion houses. But there will also be audible sighs of relief from parents and headmistresses familiar with eating disorders inspired by skinny models. Second helpings all round, girls!

---

[2] **Venus de Milo** – a famous statue of Venus, goddess of love and beauty, who had a generous figure

Jodie Kidd, a model who caused much controversy when she first appeared on the catwork

LETTERS TO THE EDITOR

Hungry and in Vogue

HOW refreshing to read that Giles Rees of Omega has withdrawn his advertising campaign from Vogue as a protest against the anorexic models they constantly promote.

As the editor and owner of the only magazine in Europe to take a positive approach to plus sizes, I find it ironic that in the three years of our existence we have never carried an advertisement of any sort other than for fashion specifically aimed at larger women.

Advertisers don't appear to believe that bigger women drive cars, wear make-up and watches, use banks or do any of the things that "normal" women do. No, we are lazy, stupid and greedy and simply sit, feeling depressed in dark corners, watching TV and eating cream cakes. (We don't get advertisements from Mr Kipling either.) Even some of the specialist chains of shops for larger women don't take ads with us in the belief that they would only be "preaching to the converted". As a very small publishing company we are swimming against an enormously strong tide of propaganda which constantly tells women they cannot live their lives unless they are thin. Not true: there are 7.5 million women in this country who are size 16 or over. Most of them are happy; many have successful careers. If Mr Rees would like to reach some of them through our advertising pages, we would be only too happy to oblige.

Janice Bhend.
Editor, Yes!
90 Banner Street,
London EC1Y 8JU.

World Press Photos of the Year

1992
DAVID C. TURNLEY
Detroit Free Press/Black Star, USA

US Sergeant Ken Kozakiewicz, 23, gives vent to his grief when he learns that the body bag at his feet contains the remains of his friend Andy Alaniz. 'Friendly fire' claimed Alaniz' life and injured Kozakiewicz. On the last day of the Gulf War they were taken away from the war zone by a MASH[3] unit evacuation helicopter.

Photographer Turnley succeeded in joining a surgical unit, which enabled him to work without being monitored. When he discovered that the army was not releasing his material, he personally retrieved it and distributed it through the news pool. Published worldwide, this picture brought home the reality of the Gulf War to millions.

[3] **MASH units** – Mobile Army Surgical Hospital units for the American military

1993
JAMES NACHTWEY
Magnum Photos, USA, for Libération, France

A mother carries her dead child to the grave in Bardera, Somalia, after wrapping it in a shroud according to local custom. A bad drought coupled with the effects of civil war caused a terrible famine in Somalia which claimed the lives of between one and two million people over a period of two years, more than 200 a day in the worst affected areas. The international airlift of relief supplies which started in July was hampered by heavily armed gangs of clansmen who looted food storage centres and slowed down the distribution of the supplies by aid organisations.

"It was the Christians"

Israeli forces had invaded Southern Lebanon on 6 June, and the PLO forces were evacuated to Syria at the end of August under American supervision. The Israelis then gave the Lebanese militia the run of the Palestinian refugee camps at Chabra and Chatila. Major Haddad was a cashiered Lebanese army officer.

John Carey

The massacre at Chatila, 16–17 September 1982

ROBERT FISK

They were everywhere, in the road, in laneways, in backyards and broken rooms, beneath crumpled masonry and across the top of garbage tips. The murderers – the Christian militiamen whom Israel had let into the camp to "flush out terrorists" fourteen hours before – had only just left. In some cases the blood was still wet on the ground. When we had seen a hundred bodies, we stopped counting.

Even twenty-four hours after the massacre of the Palestinians at Chatila had ended, no one was sure how many had been killed there. Down every alleyway there were corpses – women, young men, babies and grandparents – lying together in lazy and terrible profusion where they had been knifed or machine-gunned to death.

Each corridor through the rubble produced more bodies. The patients at a Palestine hospital simply disappeared after gunmen ordered the doctors to leave. There were signs of hastily dug mass graves. Perhaps a thousand people were butchered here, perhaps half that number again.

The full story of what happened in Chatila on Friday night and Saturday morning may never be known, for most of the witnesses are either dead or would never wish to reveal their guilt.

What is quite certain is that at six o'clock on Friday night, truckloads of gunmen in the uniform – and wearing the badges – of the right-wing Christian Phalange militia[4] and Major Saad Haddad's renegade army[5] from Southern Lebanon were seen by reporters entering the southern gate of the camp.

There were bonfires inside and the sound of heavy gunfire. Israeli troops and armour were standing round the perimeter of the camp and made no attempt to stop the gunmen – who have been their allies since their invasion of Lebanon – going in.

A spokesman for the Israeli foreign ministry was to say later that the militias had been sent into Chatila to hunt down some of the 2,000 Palestinian "terrorists" whom the Israelis alleged were still in the camp. Correspondents were forbidden to enter.

What we found inside the camp at ten o'clock next morning did not quite beggar description, although it would perhaps be easier to retell in a work of fiction or in the cold prose of a medical report.

But the details should be told for – this being Lebanon – the facts will change over the coming weeks as militias and armies and governments blame each other for the horrors committed upon the Palestinian civilians.

Just inside the southern gates of the camp, there used to be a number of single-storey, concrete-walled houses. When we walked across the muddy entrance of Chatila, we found that these buildings had all been dynamited to the ground. There were cartridge cases across the main road and clouds of flies swarmed across the rubble. Down a laneway to our right, not more than 50 yards from the entrance, there lay a pile of corpses.

There were more than a dozen of them, young men whose arms and legs had become entangled with each other in the agony of death. All had been shot at point-blank range through the right or left cheek, the bullet tearing away a line of flesh up to the ear and entering the

---

[4] **Christian Phalange militia** – army of a right-wing Christian political group in the Lebanon

[5] **regenade army** – an army which has rebelled against the people it used to support (a breakaway group)

brain. Some had vivid crimson scars down the left side of their throats. One had been castrated. Their eyes were open, and the flies had only begun to gather. The youngest was perhaps only twelve or thirteen years old.

On the other side of the main road, up a track through the rubble, we found the bodies of five women and several children. The women were middle-aged, and their corpses lay draped over a pile of rubble. One lay on her back, her dress torn open, and the head of a little girl emerging from behind her. The girl had short, dark, curly hair and her eyes were staring at us and there was a frown on her face. She was dead.

Another child lay on the roadway like a discarded flower, her white dress stained with mud and dust. She could have been no more than three years old. The back of her head had been blown away by a bullet fired into her brain. One of the women also held a tiny baby to her body. The bullet that had passed through her breast had killed the baby too.

To the right of us there was what appeared to be a small barricade of concrete and mud. But as we approached it we found a human elbow visible on the surface. A large stone turned out to be part of a torso. It was as if the bodies had been bulldozed to the side of the laneway, as indeed they had. A bulldozer – its driver's seat empty – stood guiltily just down the road.

Beyond this rampart of earth and bodies there was a pile of what might have been sacks in front of a low redstone wall. We had to cross the barricade to reach it and tried hard not to step on the bodies buried beneath.

Below the low wall a line of young men and boys lay prostrated. They had been shot in the back against the wall in a ritual execution, and they lay, at once pathetic and terrible, where they had fallen. The execution wall and its huddle of corpses was somehow reminiscent of something seen before, and only afterwards did we realise how similar it all was to those old photographs of executions in Occupied Europe during the Second World War. There may have been twelve or twenty bodies there. Some lay beneath others …

It was always the same. I found a small undamaged house with a brown metal gate leading to a small courtyard. Something instinctive made me push it open. The murderers had just left. On the ground there lay a young woman. She lay on her back as if she were sunbathing in the heat and the blood running from her back was still wet. She lay, feet together, arms outspread, as if she had seen her saviour in her last moments. Her face was peaceful, eyes closed, almost like a Madonna[6]. Only the small hole in her chest and the stain across the yard told of her death …

There had been fighting inside the camp. The road was slippery with cartridge cases and ammunition clips near the Sabra mosque[7] and some of the equipment was of the Soviet type used by the Palestinians.

There have clearly been guerrillas here. In the middle of this part of the road, however, there lay – incredibly – a perfectly carved scale-model wooden Kalashnikov[8] rifle, its barrel snapped in two. It had been a toy…

Across Chatila came the disembodied voice of an Israeli officer broadcasting through a tannoy from atop an armoured personnel carrier. "Stay off the streets," he shouted. "We are only looking for terrorists. Stay off the streets. We will shoot."

An hour later, at Galerie Semaan – far from Chatila – someone did open fire at the soldiers and I threw myself into a ditch beside an Israeli major. The Israelis fired shoals of bullets into a ruined building beside the road, blowing pieces of it into the air like confetti. The major and I lay huddled in our ditch for fifteen minutes. He asked about Chatila and I told him all I had seen.

Then he said, "I tell you this. The Haddad men were supposed to go in with us. We had to shoot two of them yesterday. We killed one and wounded another. Two more we took away. They were doing a bad thing. That is all I will tell you." Was this at Chatila? I asked. Had he been there himself? He would say no more.

Then his young radio operator, who had been lying behind us in the mud, crawled up next to me. He was a young man. He pointed to his chest. "We Israelis don't do that sort of thing," he said. "It was the Christians."

[6] **like a Madonna** – like a painting or statue of the Virgin Mary
[7] **mosque** – Muslim place of worship
[8] **Kalashnikov** – a sub-machine gun made in Russia

DAILY Mirror

Friday, September 13, 1996   **HONESTY, QUALITY, EXCELLENCE**   30p

STARTS TOMORROW
PAY OFF YOUR Mortgage

3 readers must win mortgages up to £50,000 or £40,000 cash

NatWest Collect tokens

ONE DAY TO GO...ONE DAY TO GO...ONE DAY TO GO

8 FREE £50,000 INSTANT SCRATCH CARDS

3 FREE GOES IN £10m MIRROR LOTTO SYNDICATES

DAILY **Mirror** WELCOMES YOU TO THE OPENING OF A **PAPER BAG**

Look who turned up to the opening of our paper bag

SEE PAGES 14 and 15

OASIS: NO SPLIT

BUST-UP: Noel at Heathrow yesterday

By MATTHEW WRIGHT

OASIS have NOT split up, despite the explosive end of their U.S. tour.

A furious bust-up between Noel and Liam Gallagher does not mean the end of Britain's No 1 band.

Noel, 29, flew back to London yesterday, leaving the rest of the group in the States. But insiders on the

EXCLUSIVE

tour say the band WILL re-form back in England.

They WILL finish their third album and go to Australia at the end of the year. They are still debating whether to tour Europe later this month.

The last five dates of the ill-fated

U.S. tour were scrapped after a punch-up between the feuding brothers.

A close aide said Noel blamed Liam for the tour's poor ticket sales. "There was a horrific row which ended with them coming to blows."

But Liza Markowitz, publicity director for the band's American record company Epic, confirmed: "There is no breakup."

● Full story – Pages 4 & 5

£525,000 Autumn windfall: Today's number   C 30766251

Phone Entry SEE PAGE 35

OASIS have NOT split up, despite the explosive end of their U.S. tour.

A furious bust-up between Noel and Liam Gallagher does not mean the end of Britain's No 1 band.

Noel, 29, flew back to London yesterday, leaving the rest of the group in the States. But insiders on the tour say the band **WILL** re-form back in England.

They **WILL** finish their third album and go to Australia at the end of the year. They are still debating whether to tour Europe later this month.

The last five dates of the ill-fated U.S. tour were scrapped after a punch-up between the feuding brothers.

A close aide said Noel blamed Liam for the tour's poor ticket sales. "There was a horrific row which ended with them coming to blows."

But Liza Markowitz, publicity director for the band's American record company Epic, confirmed: "There is no break-up."

And you thought twisters only hit America

By UK's Mister Twister
Prof DEREK ELSOM
*Head of Tornado Research,
Oxford Brookes University*

T'S one of the most terrifying experiences on earth.

A deafening, roaring din, like a passenger jet crashing or a 100mph train hurtling straight at you hits your ears.

It's the noise of roofs being wrenched off, power lines arcing, young trees being dragged out by their roots, mature trees being bent double until they snap and debris smashing through windows.

For most, it's only a movie. In the new Steven Spielberg blockbuster *Twister*, you can follow the American tornado trail from the edge of a cinema seat.

But the horror of a tornado can also become an awful reality – even in Britain.

Only last February, Paul and Julie Clayden and their two young children Jamie-Rose and Lee were awakened at 5.20am one day by a terrible noise.

Suddenly, violent, swirling winds wrenched off the side of their house and sucked out their first-floor window. Several other houses in Royston, Herts, suffered roof damage along a mile-long track 50 yards wide. The Claydens were victims of one of the 15 to 30 tornadoes which strike Britain each year.

The destructive power contained in these narrow, funnel-shaped clouds with their powerful, spiralling winds is awesome. But they are meat and drink to the Tornado & Research Organisation (TORRO), which uses a scale ranging from T0 to T10 to measure the intensity of twisters.

HE Claydens were lucky. Their tornado was only a T3, with 100mph winds.

The scale goes up to a nightmarish T10 – similar to the American F5 tornado rating mentioned in *Twister*.

Sheep were lifted 50ft into the air by a T5 tornado at

Pentulcae, Powys, in May 1993. The 160mph winds also sucked up hedges and fences. Frogs and fish showered from the sky when Sylvia Mowday and her two children were caught in a storm in Sutton Coldfield, West Midlands, park in June 1954.

An American tornado chase team using a portable radar has found that dust, debris and other objects lifted up into a tornado are sorted according to size by the spiralling winds. So one place is likely to get the frogs and another the pond weeds.

Passers-by were confronted by a much bigger flying object when a car was thrown 15ft into the air by a T7 tornado scything through West and North-West London later in 1954.

In 1981, Britain suffered the worst outbreak of tornadoes in Europe – 105 were triggered off in five hours as a fast-moving cold front swept across from Anglesey to East Anglia.

The earliest – and worst – recorded tornado here was the T8 twister that devastated more than 600 homes and the church at St Mary-le-Bow in London in October 1091.

At night some twisters can be eerily visible. At Dullingham, Cambs, in November 1991, Robin Hales, 15, clearly saw two large blue lights – possibly lightning – inside the rotating vortex.

Beautiful, perhaps, but it could have left death and destruction in its whirling wake.

T FOR TERROR

T0 Winds 39–54mph. Litter raised in spirals, exposed roof tiles dislodged.

T1 Winds 55–72mph. Minor damage to sheds, fences and trees.

T2 Winds 73–92mph. Light caravans blown over, garage roofs torn off.

T3 Winds 93–114mph. Caravans destroyed, garages destroyed, big trees uprooted.

T4 Winds 115–136mph. Sheds airborne, roofs removed from some houses.

T5 Winds 137–160mph. Cars lifted into the air, weaker old buildings may collapse.

T6 Winds 161–186mph. More houses collapse.

T7 Winds 187–212mph. Steel-framed buildings buckle, locomotives toppled.

T8 Winds 213–240mph. Stone houses wrecked, cars hurled long distances.

T9 Winds 241–269mph. Locomotives hurled some distance, tree trunks debarked.

T10 Winds 270mph plus. Entire frame houses lifted bodily, reinforced concrete buildings severely damaged.

She was shaking, her hands were sweating. She was trapped in a ...

WEB OF FEAR!

The nightmare story of one girl and her phobia

Words: Adelaide Dugdale

'When I opened the front door, I got the shock of my life'

A few weeks ago, I was attacked at home. I'd done a latey at work and when I opened my front door, I got the shock of my life. Behind the door – I don't know how long he'd been waiting – was an intruder. Unwanted visitors are the last thing a girl needs – especially when they're as big as this one. He was a huge figure, dressed top to toe in black. I couldn't really see his face, but he had the longest legs I'd ever seen. I imagined him overpowering me, and my legs turned to jelly.

I didn't hang around and racing upstairs, I shouted for my flatmate, 'Rachel, we've got a prowler!'

I forced her down the stairs first, cowering behind her.

'Ad, you've probably scared him away now,' said Rach. 'Where did you see him?'

'He was waiting for me behind the door as I came in,' I said.

My brave flatmate bent down and scooped something up in her hands.

'Ad-e-laide! This one's microscopic,' she said. 'When are you going to grow up and stop being afraid of spiders?'

For as long as I can remember, I've been arachnophobic. Anything with eight legs (apart from The Bluetones, that is) makes me quake with fear. And I was stupid enough to mention this in the office.

'Aah, so you've got a phobia?' said our Ed, stroking her chin.

Me and my big mouth.

In therapy!

So, it is with a heavy heart and shaky legs that I find myself at London Zoo for the Friendly

Spider Programme. Run by a hypnotherapist, Robert Farrago, the course promises to cure you of your arachnophobia in just over three hours.

Before now I've tried every cure known to man – my friends, family and boyfriends always try to sort me out. They just don't understand that I don't really care about being scared of spiders. I'm only worried the moment I come face to face with one.

A friend of mine took me to the movie *Arachnophobia* in an attempt to sort me out for good.

'Look, Adelaide, it's only a pretend spider. Ad? Ad? Come out from under the seat. You haven't got to the good bit yet.'

And then there was the ex who kept a live spider in a jam jar by his bed. Every time I got too cheeky, he would threaten me with it. He didn't last long!

Back in the zoo's meeting room, there are 30 of us milling around – including several men. Anyone who thinks that being phobic is girly-wuss behaviour is totally WRONG. I saw one bloke checking for cobwebs under his chair. Everyone here is very nervous – and can you blame us? At the end of the three hour session, we've got to meet Freda and Charlotte, the zoo's resident Mexican red-kneed, bird-eating spiders. I can't believe I'm doing this! First of all there's a few hours of spider speak. I just hope I can get through the mere mention of the word 'spider' without passing out. Here goes …

Spider speak

First of all, Doctor Robert explains to us exactly what a phobia is. Basically, it's what happens when the subconscious part of your brain reacts before you've had time to think.

Having established that, we get down to the rather more daunting task of working out what it is about the beasts that turn us into a wobbling bowl of Chivers.

'The legs. There are too many of them and they move so quickly,' pipes up someone from the back of the room. Yup, I can appreciate that one.

Then it's my turn. 'Whenever I see a spider, all I can think about is, "What if it were the same size as me?"' I say.

The room erupts, and

Robert says, 'You should go to Birmingham – there's a museum with a 50 foot spider in a case.' I make a mental note never to visit my parents (Brummies and proud) again.

We spend an hour discussing everything there is to discuss about spiders and what happens to us when we see one. Everyone has pretty much the same reaction: racing heart, rooted to the spot, hyperventilating and adrenaline rush. One woman said that if she sees one before bedtime, she'll sleep with the light on. Robert assured us that no spider can kill a person. Phew! That's a relief then.

Then it's on to what we should do when we actually come face to face with a spider. 'Kill and dismember it,' screeches someone.

'Get someone else to stamp on it.'

'Set the dog or cat on it!' shout the others. The serving suggestion du jour, however, is boil-in-the-bag spider. All you do is scoop the beast into a plastic bag and drop it in a pan of boiling water. Simple, if you can bear to get that close to it!

Hypno heaven

Next, there's a party political broadcast by the Spiders For Life Party. Paul, the zoo's chief spiderman, arrives and gives us a potted history of spiders. After a while you can't help but admire the little critters – and feel embarrassment about being frightened by something that's the size of a bogey with half the intelligence. According to Paul, 'Spiders don't think, because they can't!' Aaah!

After tea and biscuits, the group sits in silence and ponders which vegetables to serve with boil-in-the-bag spider! Everyone's trying not to think about the touchy-feely spiderama moment, which is looming large. Firstly, however, it's hypnotherapy time. Robert orders us all to sit on the floor and concentrate on a spot on the ceiling. Then he's away with his manic banter and before we know it, our eyes have closed, our heads are lolling and we're probably dribbling onto our collars.

I can't remember much about this bit, but I saw some pretty spooky things. Robert counted us down into a trance by making us mentally walk down ten steps. When we reached the bottom, he told us, we would enter a hypnotic state. Suddenly, I was swimming through the bluest ocean I've ever seen. Everything was so real – I could still hear his voice, but my mind was about three thousand miles away on a Caribbean island. I journeyed through puffs of purple and green mist, until I was flying miles above white billowy clouds. Bliss.

The crunch!

I vaguely remember Robert urging us to put all our phobias about 'spiders into that cloud and watch it turn black'. We then had to mentally 'blow it away and watch our fears disappear with it'. He then snapped us out of the trance.

No prizes for what my first thought was. Yup, spiders. It was time for us to meet genuine web-spinners. My knickers were heading for a twist situation!

Paul had brought us Freda and Charlotte, his furry friends, to cuddle. Some people rushed over for a free fondle, but not me! It took me ten minutes to just get over to the table.

I'm not sure that it was the hypnotherapy that cured my fear of spiders, but the info I'd been fed before helped. I felt like a bully, who'd been picking on the weakest girl in school. But the real turning point came when Freda and Charlotte were brought out and everyone had a chance to see the monsters close up! The biggest shock was that they weren't really monsters – Charlotte was the most beautiful spider I'd ever seen. Her coat – yes, I stroked it – was really warm and velvety. I spent five minutes holding her, and I didn't want to give her back.

I've definitely cured my phobia. The course even taught me how to 'capture and release' a spider. That's when you trap the offending octoped in a jam jar, slide a piece of paper over the top and then release it outside. Their exit from my flat used to be via the plughole with a gallon of water.

I can't promise that a spider will never suffer at my hands again, but I can guarantee Rach will never be dragged out of bed at 4am.

'After a bit, I couldn't help but admire the little critters'

Journo-lists

1

Pub grub – a guide to interpretation

★ 'Traditional menu': Chips with everything
★ 'Vegetarian special': Salad
★ 'Tasty jacket potato': We've got a microwave!
★ 'Garnish': Single, limp lettuce leaf (re-usable)
★ 'Chilli con carne': Shepherd's pie without the potato topping
★ 'Today's special': Yesterday's leftovers
★ 'Ploughman's lunch': Bank clerk's lunch
★ 'Gateau': Sponge cake with a hefty price tag
★ 'Soup of the day': Soup of the week
★ 'Cooked to your requirements': Over-cooked to our specifications

2

'It's only a phase ... ' – ten stages teenagers go through

★ Looking at their reflection in every shop window they pass
★ Giving up breakfast
★ Pretending not to be with the family when on holiday
★ Being bored with everything
★ Staying in bed until noon
★ Keeping a diary
★ Clothes shopping at jumble sales
★ Communicating in monosyllables
★ Displaying an extraordinary talent for secrecy
★ Going vegetarian

Advertising and publicity

Advertising works by trying to connect some of our everyday needs and wishes to a product that the advertiser wants to sell – perhaps material needs, like our need to be fed, clothed and healthy, or psychological needs, such as our desire to be loved, successful or admired.

This selection contains ads for Lamplough's Pyretic Saline (1884), Horlicks (1951), Lucozade (1995), Benetton (1989) and S-Curl (1996). They all appeared in newspapers or magazines or on posters or TV. None of them simply tell us the name of the product. All try to convince us that we would be better off if we bought them.

There are also two examples of modern publicity leaflets: an appeal for donations to Amnesty International, a charity which tries to end abuses of human rights, and an invitation to follow a nature trail at Bradwell Power Station.

Folio of ads: 1884–1996

the moon, darling?

D'you want the moon, I said! I was so sure I was going to succeed. But I couldn't concentrate, couldn't think. That little outing of mine put the lid on it – and I went to see the doctor. He told me about how sleep must reach down into the subconscious – and how Horlicks would help me get **profound** sleep! Horlicks made quite a difference – success feels pretty good!

HORLICKS

THE GREAT REMEDY

For INDIGESTION, HEADACHE,
BILIOUSNESS [9], FEVERS, AND CHOLERA.

Drs. PROUT, MORGAN, TURLEY, GIBBON, SPARKS, DOWSING, STEVENS, and many other Medical Gentlemen, have given unqualified testimony to the importance of the discovery and the great value of **LAMPLOUGH'S PYRETIC SALINE** as possessing elements most essential to the restoration and maintenance of Health with perfect vigour of Body and Mind. It is Effervescing and Tasteless, forming a most **Invigorating, Vitalising and Refreshing Beverage**.

Gives instant relief in **Headache, Sea or Bilious Sickness, Constipation, Indigestion, Lassitude**[10], **Heartburn**, and **Feverish Colds**; prevents and quickly cures the worst form of **Typhus**, **Scarlet** and other **Fevers**, **Smallpox**, **Measles**, and **Eruptive** or **Skin Complaints**, and various other altered conditions of the Blood.

CAUTION.– *Beware of Spurious Salines and Effervescing Salts containing injurious elements, put forward by unprincipled persons as the same or better thing.*

In patent Glass-Stoppered Bottles, **2s. 6d., 4s. 6d., 11s.** and **21s.** each. *To be obtained of any Chemist or Patent Medicine Dealer, and of*

H. LAMPLOUGH, 113, Holborn, London, E.C.

[9] **biliousness** – a feeling of sickness
[10] **lassitude** – physical or mental tiredness

Script

Revision Number: 1

Client: SmithKline Beecham
Product: Lucozade Sport
Length: 30 seconds   TV/Cinema: TV
Title: Premier League II   Date: 22.2.95

MUSIC: ROCK TRACK THROUGHOUT

Open on an overhead shot of attacker taking on a defender.
Cut to a player juggling the ball over the heads of opponents.

TITLE: SKILL (The 'i's in all the titles are formed by a Lucozade Sport can.)

An attacker bearing down on goal is tackled by two defenders.
A dramatic sliding tackle.
Cut to a player sidestepping a tackle.
Two more players being tackled in quick succession.

TITLE: GRIT

Two shots of different players shouting in close-up.

TITLE: DRIVE

Cut to a wide shot of a player shooting at goal. Then a forward heading at goal. Another shot of a player shooting followed by a free kick swerving shot.

TITLE: STRIKE

A player celebrates scoring by doing a back flip.
Five quick shots of players celebrating.

TITLE: PASSION

Shot of crowd cheering followed by player curling a shot into the goal.

TITLE: OFFICIAL SPORTS DRINK

Shot of crowd cheering and jumping up and down.

TITLE: (PREMIER LEAGUE LOGO)

Final shot of a player drinking from a plastic bottle.

END TITLE: ISOTONIC

Script by Ogilvy & Mather

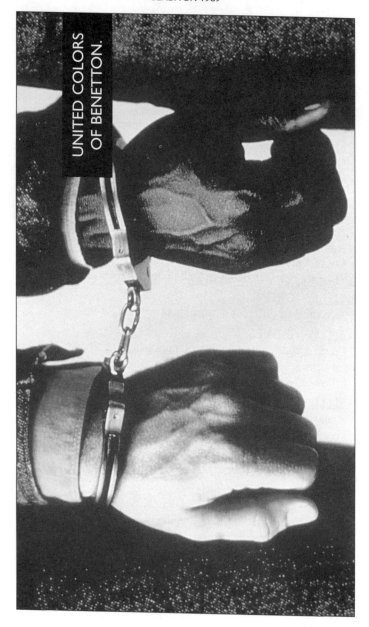

UNITED COLORS
OF BENETTON.

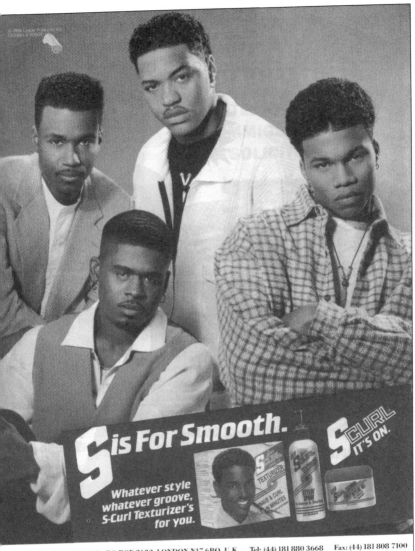

MURDERERS TORTURERS RAPISTS

'I know what I'd like to say to them. Do you?'
Award-winning journalist, John Pilger.

Dear Friend,

For years, the former Soviet Union, the USA and its European allies, as well as China, Pakistan, Saudi Arabia, Egypt and Iran, allowed weapons to pour into Afghanistan. Did they stop to think about who their guns and missiles would be used by, or against?

When 80 ordinary civilians were blown to bits as they waited at a bus stop in Kabul, did the arms suppliers worry about who had supplied the missiles?

Did they apologise to the young man and woman who, minutes after their brother's wedding, found themselves scrabbling through the dead and torn bodies of their relatives after a warring faction 'got their own back'?

Did they ask about the guns held to prisoners' heads to force them to eat what their captors told them was human flesh? And did they wonder about the victims who were killed to supply this gruesome meal?

Did they concern themselves about the young woman abducted in Kabul and then raped at gunpoint by <u>22 men for three days?</u> Did they have to listen to her screams when she got home to discover her three little children dead from hypothermia?

Did they say sorry to the man who had a machine gun stuck in his face when he tried to take his wife, who was in labour, to hospital? Did they go with him to collect her dead body and that of his newborn baby? Can they help him understand that they died from lack of medical care just because a group of men with guns decided it would be fun to watch a baby being born?

<u>I'm sure you will be stunned into silence by these appalling tragedies. I've worked as a researcher for Amnesty International for ten years, yet even I was speechless when the families of those who suffered these abuses told me their stories.</u>

But to remain silent is the <u>last thing</u> the people of Afghanistan want us to do.

<u>The world has kept quiet for too long.</u>

Since the Soviets left in 1989, and the situation deteriorated into a bloody and bitter civil war amongst uncontrollable rival factions, the world powers have been trying to wash their hands of the mess that is now Afghanistan.

<u>But the blood of thousands of innocent lives is not so easily washed off.</u>

With <u>your</u> help, Amnesty International has been speaking up for the people of Afghanistan. We've put the pressure on where it counts. We've lobbied, argued and protested. In November 1995 we began a campaign for a resolution on Afghanistan which was passed in the European Parliament in January 1996. The first one for *four* years. People <u>are</u> listening to us.

Thanks to your support for us, it's getting harder and harder for those who had a hand in fuelling the Afghan war to deny responsibility for the grotesque human rights catastrophe that is now taking place. So far they've managed to remain silent.

<u>But not for much longer.</u>

We are determined to get <u>every</u> nation involved to admit that those who are committing human rights atrocities in Afghanistan now, only got to their positions of power with *their* help, *their* guns, *their* money.

The only way to get them to listen to us is to MAKE A NOISE and raise the roof on human rights abuses in Afghanistan. To do that we have to raise *our* voice much louder than ever before, <u>which means raising more funds than ever before too.</u>

The UK Section recently faced having to cut back on vital campaigns including Afghanistan. But thanks to the support of committed people like you, we now have the chance to redress the balance.

Can you help us? Send a donation for as much as you can afford to our appeal now and we'll use it to KEEP ON RESEARCHING AND SPEAKING OUT ABOUT HUMAN RIGHTS ABUSES UNTIL SOMETHING IS DONE!

And by dialling 0990 133 370 NOW, YOU can support our appeal AND speak out with us! We're sending a taped message to every nation responsible for Afghanistan's plight. Add your voice to it!

Tell them you're supporting Amnesty International with a donation because you want to see respect for human rights restored in Afghanistan. Tell those who are still supplying arms to obtain guarantees that they are not used to commit or facilitate human rights abuses. Tell them to bring all their pressure to bear to get the warring factions within the country to stop their atrocities.

YOU can save lives in Afghanistan by supporting Amnesty International and speaking out NOW!

Yours sincerely,

Abbas Faiz
Researcher
Asia & Pacific Regional Program

AMNESTY
INTERNATIONAL
UNITED KINGDOM

Bradwell nature trail's flora and fauna...

Welcome to Bradwell power station's nature trail! We aim to show you just how we have ensured that man's activities can fit in with nature and the environment.

Bradwell and nature – Partners

The Bradwell nature trail is the ideal location for schoolchildren to carry out science and nature projects. We welcome children of all ages on to our trail to explore many different habitats ranging from a track and wood to a pond and beach.

We can provide classroom facilities to meet the needs of younger guests – you can combine a tour of the power station and visitor centre with a nature ramble.

Visitor centre opening hours

Open 1000 hours to 1600 hours every day during the Summer. Off season, closed Saturdays.

Admission is FREE

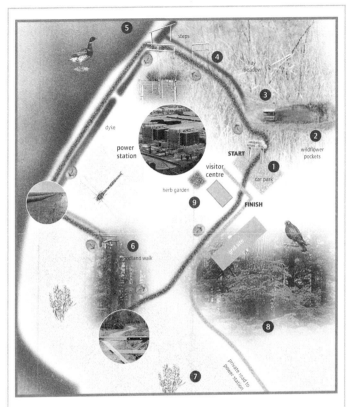

1 Work started on the Bradwell nature trail in mid 1994 in parallel with the building of the visitor centre. It was opened officially in May 1995 by Chris Packham – presenter of the 'Really Wild Show'.

Walking time is approximately one hour – stout shoes are advisable. Please observe the country code.

2 This area has been planted with **wild flower pockets**. Numerous species such as Sweet Rocket, Corn Marigold, Honesty and Honeysuckle can be found here.

3 The **dipping pond** was dug in 1994. School children can study the aquatic plants and animals which are now established. You will see signs of Water Boatmen, Pond Skaters, Frogs, Newts, Dragons and Sticklebacks.

4 Follow the trail alongside the **hay meadow**. You will see a coppice planted by local school children in 1995 to celebrate National Tree Week.

5 **The Blackwater Estuary** has been important for wildlife for many thousands of years. It is particularly valuable for its wintering and passage wildfowl and waders.

The estuary has internationally important numbers of Brent Geese, Shelduck, Oystercatcher, Ringed Plover, Grey Plover, Dunlin, Knot, Bartailed Godwit, Redshank, Curlew and Turnstone.

The coastal zone which includes the borrow dyke, sea wall, saltmarsh and foreshore, is all part of two Sites of Special Scientific Interest (SSSI).

Warning! Please be careful on the beach – the sand is covering thick deep mud.

6 Climb over the stile and you will enter our **woodland walk** where native broadleaf trees such as Cherry Oak, Sorbus, and Birch have been planted.

7 Much of the non operational land is under intensive **agriculture**. Crops of winter wheat, lucerne, linseed, and oilseed rape are regularly harvested.

8 To the south of the station are three Corsican **pine plantations** planted on raised banks. This helps to screen views of the power station. This habitat is also home to nesting birds and small mammals.

9 The **herb garden** is the latest addition to the nature trail. It is of traditional style and all herbs will be used for educational purposes.

Where to find us

Radio

Radio is the simplest medium in this book. It directs itself just to one sense: hearing. The writer Andrew Crisell says that '... it is a *blind* medium. We cannot see its messages, they consist only of noise and silence, and it is from the sole fact of its blindness that all radio's other distinctive qualities – the nature of its language, its jokes, the way in which its audience uses it – ultimately derive.'

These three examples of radio make particular use of the radio medium by emphasising speech, sounds, music and silence.

Jane Eyre

by Charlotte Brontë
Dramatised by Michelene Wandor

Episode 1 Jane, the child

Scene 1

Sweep of wind, with distant musical rumble.

JANE   A dreary November day. A cold winter wind. A pale bank of mist and cloud. Wet lawn. Storm-beaten shrubbery. Ceaseless rain. Sweeping, sweeping, sweeping.

Music fades up.

There is no possibility of taking a walk today.

Music up further.

ANNOUNCER   Jane Eyre, by Charlotte Brontë. Dramatised for radio in four episodes by Michelene Wandor. Episode One: Jane, the child.

Music continues. Door slams shut, on echo acoustic.

JOHN   (*Age 14, on same acoustic*) Animal! Where have you gone? Oh dear. The creature must have run out into the garden. Bad thing.

Sound of curtain being violently drawn. JANE *gasps. Music stops. Drawing room.*

Why, here you are. Hiding again. And you are reading. How dare you.

36

JOHN *slaps* JANE.

JANE   Ow. You are a cruel boy. I hate you.

JOHN   Do not answer back. Give me that book.

JANE   I am reading it.

JOHN   Do not answer back. Give me that book.

JANE   I am reading it.

JOHN   Mama says you are a dependent. You have no business to read our books. You ought to beg, and not live here with gentlemen's children like us and eat the same meals we do and wear clothes at our expense.

JANE   You are wicked, like the Roman emperors.

JOHN   Wicked, you say. We shall see. There.

JOHN *pulls her hair.*

JANE   Let go of my hair. Ow!

JOHN   Rat. Nasty, stupid rat. You are a beast and a beggar.

Shouting and hitting, JANE *sobbing,* JOHN *yelling.*

JANE   (*Sobbing*) I hate you, I hate you.

JOHN   Help. The animal is attacking me. Help. Help.

He screams.
Door opens

MRS REED   (*Approaching*) Well, I never. Bessie, Bessie, come quickly. Oh, my poor John.

Scuffle continues

JOHN   Mama, mama –

MRS REED   Stop it at once. John, darling – oh, she is mad. Bessie. Hurry.

BESSIE   (*Arriving*) What is – oh, Lord. Dear, dear, what a fury to fly at master John. Come here, Miss Jane.

MRS REED   Take her to the red room and lock her in.

JANE   You shan't touch me.

BESSIE   Now come along, Miss Jane.

    JANE *screams.*

MRS REED   Hold her. She's like a mad cat.

JANE   I hate you. I hate you all.

BESSIE   Quiet now, Miss Jane.

JANE   I would be warmer in the middle of frost and snow. I would be happier in a graveyard than at the tea-table here. I hate you all.

    Sobbing, into distort

Scene 2

    Int. door closes. Red room. JANE *sobs quietly.*

BESSIE   For shame, Miss Eyre. To strike a young gentleman, your young master.

JANE   How is he my master? I'm not a servant.

BESSIE   You are less than a servant, for you do nothing for your keep. Now you must be a good girl and think over your wickedness.

JANE   I am not wicked.

BESSIE   You must be aware that you are under obligations to Mrs Reed. If she were to turn you out, you would have to go to the poorhouse. You should be useful and pleasant.

JANE   I hate Mrs Reed. And I hate John Reed.

BESSIE   God will punish you, Miss Jane. What have you to say?

JANE   Nothing.

BESSIE   Well, I will leave you to repent your wickedness. Say your prayers, child.

JANE   Oh, Bessie, don't leave me alone. I do not hate you.

BESSIE   (*Footsteps leaving*) You must think about your sins.

Door closes

JANE Bessie. (JANE *sobs*)

Music

(*Over*) This is the red room.

BERTHA (*Whisper, on echo*) Red room.

JANE The carpet is red, the table at the foot of the bed is covered with a crimson cloth. The two large windows have their blinds always drawn down. It was in this chamber that Mr Reed breathed his last, Bertha. Here he lay, and from here his coffin was borne by the undertaker's men.

BERTHA (*Sighs*)

JANE The room is chilly. (JANE *begins to move around*) By the window, a large looking-glass. (*She gasps*) What a pale face. What glittering eyes. Is that me? Is that Jane Eyre?

BERTHA (*Whisper*) Jane. Jane.

JANE Why do they always think me naughty?

BERTHA Jane Eyre, Jane Eyre.

JANE My head aches. Why can I never please?

BERTHA (*Whisper*) Please.

JANE No one dares thwart John, even though he twists the necks of the pigeons and he sets dogs at the sheep. It will be dark soon.

BERTHA Dark.

Wind

JANE Perhaps I am wicked. Perhaps they will forget me and I shall starve to death here.

BERTHA Wicked.

JANE Mr Reed would have treated me kindly. Perhaps he will revisit the earth to punish the wrong and avenge the oppressed. Perhaps his spirit will arise before me like a ghost.

BERTHA Ghost, Jane. (*Laughter*)

Wind louder

JANE (*Screams*) What is that?

BERTHA Dark. No moon.

JANE *screams. Rattles doorknob*

JANE Take me out.

BERTHA Dark.

JANE I want to go into the nursery. Bessie. Bessie, come quickly. I do not want to stay here.

BERTHA Stay here.

JANE (*Screaming with terror*) Aunt Reed, have pity. Forgive me. I am sorry.

BERTHA Stay. Stay.

JANE Do not leave me here – I cannot bear it –

Footsteps outside and key turns in lock.

Bessie – oh, Bessie. (JANE *screams and faints*)

Music

Scene 3

Int. nursery.

JANE (*Waking*) Bessie?

BESSIE Here, Miss Jane.

JANE What is that fire?

BESSIE It is only the nursery fire.

JANE My head hurts.

BESSIE I will shade the candle.

LLOYD How are you feeling?

JANE Who is that?

BESSIE It is Mr Lloyd, the apothecary.

JANE Why? What is the matter with me?

40

LLOYD   You fell sick in the red room, with crying. Bessie, fetch her something to eat.

JANE   Bessie –

BESSIE   I will not be long.

Door closes softly.

LLOYD   Well, now. Why do you cry so much, Miss Jane Eyre?

JANE   I cry because I am miserable.

LLOYD   And why are you miserable?

JANE   I was shut up in a room where there is a ghost. No one will go into the red room at night, and it was cruel to shut me up alone without a candle.

LLOYD   Are you afraid now in daylight?

JANE   No. Now I am just unhappy.

LLOYD   But why? Gateshead Hall is a very beautiful house. Are you not very thankful to have such a fine place to live at?

JANE   Bessie says I have less right to be here than the servants.

LLOYD   Have you any other relations?

JANE   I don't know. I asked Aunt Reed once and she said I might have some poor low relations called Eyre that she knew nothing about.

LLOYD   If you have such, would you like to go to them?

JANE   No. I should not like to belong to poor people.

LLOYD   Not even if they were kind to you?

JANE   No. I do not think so.

LLOYD   Would you like to go to school?

JANE   I think I should like to go to school. Bessie says they have paintings and landscapes. They sing songs and translate French books.

LLOYD   You enjoy reading?

Door opens

JANE   Oh, yes.

BESSIE   (*Approaching*) Here we are. A bun and some cheesecake. And your favourite plate, with the bird of paradise on it.

JANE   Thank you, Bessie. You are the kindest being in the world. (JANE *eats*)

LLOYD   I will leave you now, Jane.

JANE   Goodbye, Mr Lloyd.

LLOYD   (*Low*) Bessie – walk to the door with me.

Footsteps to the door

Goodbye, Jane.

Door opens, closes and they walk in corridor.

How did the child come here?

BESSIE   Her father was a poor clergyman, and her mother married him against the wishes of his friends. Her grandfather Reed cut her off without a shilling. After they had been married a year her father caught the typhus fever. Her mother took the infection from him and they died within a month of each other. Poor Miss Jane.

LLOYD   Indeed.

Footsteps fade

Scene 4

Music
Carriage mixes with music
Knock on door cuts off all other effects. Door opens.
Drawing room

MRS REED   Ah. Come in, child. This is the little girl respecting whom I applied to you, Mr Brocklehurst.

MR B.   She is very small. What is her age?

MRS REED   Ten years.

MR B. What is your name, little girl?

JANE Jane Eyre, sir.

MR B. Well, Jane Eyre. Are you a good child?

MRS REED Perhaps the less said on that subject the better, Mr Brocklehurst.

MR B. I'm sorry indeed to hear it. Come here, child. Do you know where the wicked go after death?

JANE They go to hell, sir.

MR B. And what is hell?

JANE A pit full of fire.

MR B. And should you like to fall into that pit and to be burning there for ever.

JANE No, sir.

MR B. What must you do to avoid it?

JANE I must keep in good health and not die. (*She sighs*)

MRS REED You see?

MR B. I hope that sigh is from the heart, child, and that you repent of ever having been the occasion of discomfort to your excellent benefactress. Do you say your prayers? Night and morning?

JANE Yes, sir.

MR B. Do you read your Bible?

JANE Sometimes.

MR B. That proves you have a wicked heart. You must pray to God to change it to take away your heart of stone and give you a new and clean one.

JANE How is my heart to be changed? It is in my body.

MRS REED Mr Brocklehurst. I believe I intimated in my letter that this little girl has not quite the character and disposition I could wish. Should you admit her to Lowood School, I should be glad if the superintendent and teachers were requested to keep a strict eye on her, and above all to guard against her worst fault, a tendency to deceit. I mention this in your hearing, Jane, that you may not attempt to impose on Mr Brocklehurst.

JANE Mrs Reed, it is in your nature to wound me cruelly. I have never been happy in your presence. However much I strive to obey, my efforts are always repulsed.

MR B. Deceit is a sad fault in a child. It is akin to falsehood, and all liars will have their portion in the lake burning with fire and brimstone. She shall be watched, Mrs Reed.

MRS REED As for the vacations, she will, with your permission, spend them always at Lowood.

MR B. Indeed, Mrs Reed.

MRS REED Consistency, my dear Mr Brocklehurst. I advocate consistency in all things.

MR B. Consistency, madam, is the first of Christian duties, and it has been observed in every arrangement connected with the establishment of Lowood. Plain fare, simple attire, unsophisticated accommodation, hardy and active habits, such is the order of the day in the house and its inhabitants.

MRS REED Quite right, sir. I may then depend upon this child being received as a pupil at Lowood.

MR.B Madam, you may. And I trust she will show herself grateful.

MRS REED I will send her as soon as possible. I am anxious to be relieved of a responsibility that is becoming irksome.

MR B. I shall send Miss Temple notice that she is to expect a new girl. Goodbye, Mrs Reed.

MRS REED Goodbye, Mr Brocklehurst. Jane?

JANE Goodbye, Mr Brocklehurst.

Door closes. In the course of the following the carriage leaves in the background. Clock ticks. Silence, briefly

MRS REED You may return to the nursery, Jane.

JANE   I am not deceitful. If I were, I should say I loved you, but I declare I do not love you. I dislike you the worst of anybody in the world except John Reed.

MRS REED   Well, I never did.

JANE   I will never call you aunt again as long as I live. I will never come to see you when I am grown up, and if anyone asks me how I liked you and how you treated me I will say that you treated me with miserable cruelty, and the very thought of you makes me sick.

MRS REED   How dare you affirm that, Jane Eyre.

JANE   Because it is the truth. You think I have no feelings and that I can do without one bit of love or kindness. But I cannot live so. And you have no pity. I shall remember until my dying day how you threw me into the red room and locked me up there. People think you are a good woman, but you are bad and hard-hearted.

MRS REED   Jane, what is the matter with you? I assure you I desire to be your friend.

JANE   You told Mr Brocklehurst I had a bad character, a deceitful disposition.

MRS REED   Jane, you do not understand. Children must be corrected for their faults.

JANE   Deceit is not my fault.

MRS REED   But you are passionate, Jane. That you must allow. Now return to the nursery, there's a dear, and lie down a little.

JANE   I am not your dear. I cannot lie down. Send me to school soon, Mrs Reed, for I hate to live here.

Door slams.

Sunday Afternoon at Home

HANCOCK'S HALF-HOUR
by Ray Galton and Alan Simpson
Broadcast: 22 April 1958

TONY (*Yawns*) Oh dear. Oh dear oh dear. Cor dear me. Stone me, what a life. What's the time?

BILL Two o'clock.

TONY Is that all? Cor dear oh dear me. I don't know. (*Yawns*) Oh, I'm fed up.

SIDNEY Oi.

TONY What?

SIDNEY Why don't you shut up moaning and let me get on with the paper?

TONY Well, I'm fed up.

SIDNEY So you just said.

TONY Well, so I am.

SIDNEY Look, so am I fed up, and so is Bill fed up. We're all fed up, so shut up moaning and make the best of it.

TONY Are you sure it's only two o'clock?

BILL No, it's er … one minute past two now.

TONY One minute past two. Doesn't the time drag? Ooh I do hate Sundays. I'll be glad when it's over. It drives me up the wall just sitting here looking at you lot. Every Sunday it's the same. Nowhere to go, nothing to do. Just sit here waiting for the next lot of grub to come up. There must be something we can do. Bill, haven't you got any bright ideas?

BILL No.

TONY It was a waste of time asking really, wasn't it? (*Pause. Yawns*) Oh I'm fed up.

HATTIE Why don't you men go out for a walk while I wash up the dishes?

TONY (*Mimics her*) 'Why don't you men go for a walk?' Why don't *you* go for a walk? Go on, hoppit. It'll be one less to look at all day. (*Pause*) Have you finished with that paper yet?

SIDNEY No.

TONY Well hurry up, I haven't seen it yet. I want to know what my stars say.

SIDNEY What are you?

TONY June the twenty-first.

SIDNEY What sign is that?

HATTIE The crab.

TONY And what of it?

HATTIE I didn't say anything.

TONY The delight with which you said it implied an opinion. Watch it. I can't help being a crab. I had no choice about which day I should be born on; the matter was entirely out of my hands. I could easily have been a Leo, or a Gemini, or even an Aquarium, but fate decreed that I should be a crab.

SIDNEY Cancer the Crab, where are we? … Ah, here it is.

TONY What does it say?

SIDNEY It says, 'Today looks like being a very exciting day'.

TONY Well, good luck to him. Who is he? Arnold the Gipsy. Look at him, spotted handkerchief round his head, great cartwheel ear-rings. A right fake if ever I saw one. The nearest he's been to a caravan was at the Motor Show. Very exciting day indeed. Two o'clock gone and what's happened? The cat ran away with a sardine. The milkman left only one pint instead of two, and Mrs Crevatte next door crept home at nine o'clock this morning after being out all night. Moments of high drama all that lot. What's going to happen next? The tension's killing me.

SIDNEY Why don't you turn it in?

Pause. A few clearing of throats, sighs, etc.

HATTIE Oh look, it's started raining.

TONY That's all we wanted. You watch, it'll go dark in a minute and we'll have to switch the lights on.
I think I'll go to bed.

HATTIE You've only been up an hour!

TONY That's by the way and nothing to do with it. I might just as well be in bed: there's nothing else to do.
I wish I hadn't got up now. Your dinner wasn't worth getting up for, I'll tell you that. Sunday dinner is usually the meal of the week, the one thing that makes Sunday bearable. But not here. On Sundays in this house we get the same rubbish as the rest of the week, dished up on the best china, that's all.

HATTIE What was wrong with the dinner?

TONY Now be honest, it wasn't very good, was it?

HATTIE Well I don't know, I ate all mine.

TONY That's neither here nor there. You also ate Bill's, Sid's and mine. How you got your teeth through that roast beef I shall never know. I can only assume you sharpened them up on the Yorkshire Pudding.

HATTIE It wasn't my fault, it was frozen meat.

TONY That joint was harder when you took it out of the oven than when you put it in. That meal, whichever way you look at it, was a complete fiasco. I thought my mother was a bad cook, but at least her gravy used to move about. Yours just lays there and sets.

HATTIE That's the goodness in it.

TONY That's the half-pound of flour you put in it! I saw you shovel it in there; I thought you were going to plaster the room out. There's something wrong when you have to ask for another slice of gravy. It's not right.

48

SIDNEY Here, there's a bloke here who can cure gallstones by just putting his hands on your forehead.

BILL That's a funny place to have gallstones.

SIDNEY No, no. He's got a box, you see, and he transmits life waves. You see, everybody's got life waves, and it says here this box tunes into your life waves and the waves travel through his fingertips into your forehead and smash your gallstones up.

TONY Charming.

SIDNEY Well, it makes you think, don't it? He says he can cure anything so long as he gets on the right wavelength.

TONY I know, and for an extra five bob he'll tune your earholes into Family Favourites[11]. What a load of rubbish. You don't believe everything you read in a Sunday newspaper, do you? I would have thought you had more intelligence. It's a lot of silly nonsense. I find it incredible that after thousands of years of civilisation, we, in this day and age, in the twentieth century, still find ourselves surrounded by silly superstitious nonsense swallowed avidly by supposedly educated, intelligent beings. Bill, what do my stars say in your paper?

BILL Huh? Mmmmm?

TONY What are you doing pressing your stomach in?

BILL I've been thinking about these gallstones. I think I've got them.

TONY How do you know?

BILL Well look, you feel. I've got two bumps, see. One just here and one round there.

TONY Lift your pullover up. You buffoon. They're the metal bits on your braces. Great oaf. I was asking

[11] **Family Favourites** – a popular BBC radio programme of the 1950s and 60s which played listeners' musical requests

you what my stars say in your paper. Romany Jim on
page four.

BILL It's not here. I tore that bit out to put in the toe of
my shoe because it's too big.

TONY There's all yesterday's papers to do that with, but
no. You have to tear out Romany Jim. I want to
know what he said. Take your shoe off.

SIDNEY You've heard what Arnold the Gipsy said.

TONY I've got no faith in Arnold the Gipsy. I want a
second opinion.

BILL Well you can't have it. I'm not taking my shoe off.

SIDNEY Why don't you sit down and relax. It's a day of rest.
Have a kip or something, anything, but do me a
favour and shut up. Here, have a couple of pages of
my paper. I'll keep the racing results and the
gallstone smasher; you can have the court cases and
the woman's page.

TONY Oh dear. What a life. It's Sunday, I've had a rotten
dinner, it's raining, Romany Jim's been torn up and
I've got nothing to do.

HATTIE There's plenty of odd jobs you can do around the
house.

TONY Oh shut up. It's a day of rest. I'm not mending your
bed again.

SIDNEY (*Wearily*) Read the paper, will you?

TONY Well … it makes you sick. I hate Sundays.

SIDNEY So do I, but there's one a week, there always has
been, and there's nothing we can do about it.

TONY It's not like this on the continent, it's their big day
over there. All the cafes open, football matches,
race meetings, everybody's gay. Not over here
though. Everything's shut up.

SIDNEY I wish you would.

Long pause. Clearing throats. Humming. Sighs. Papers rustling.

TONY Get your feet out of the way, put them over there.

Pause.

That's it, go on, take all the fire up. Don't let anyone else get a look at it, will you?

HATTIE I'm sorry, I'm just trying to get warm.

Pause.

TONY What's the time?

BILL Er ... the little hand's on two and the big hand's on three. That's ... er ... three minutes past two.

TONY It is a quarter past two.

BILL Oh yeah, that's right.

TONY Quarter past two. Another nine and three-quarter hours before it's Monday. Depressing, isn't it? I don't care very much for Mondays either. And me Saturdays are always spoilt thinking about Sunday. You know, I sometimes think, what's it all about? What are we here for? Don't you sometimes think that?

BILL No.

TONY No, of course not.

Pause. TONY *smacks his lips. Sighs. Hums a bit.*

SIDNEY Here. He can get rid of malaria as well.

TONY Who can?

SIDNEY The bloke with the radio set. It says Mr D of Huddersfield had malaria for years, but this bloke tuned into his wavelength, switched on, put his hands on his forehead, and it was gone.

TONY How very interesting.

SIDNEY It makes you think, though, don't it?

Long pause. Rustle of newspaper. Little bit of singing from TONY *which tails off and dies away into an embarrassed silence. Pause*

TONY Have you noticed, when you look at that wallpaper long enough you can see faces on it?

BILL Honest?

TONY Yes, yes you can, you can see faces after a time. It's the pattern, it makes little faces. There's a lovely one of an old man with a pipe.

BILL Where?

TONY Come over here. Look at it from where I'm sitting. Screw your eyes up, now stare hard, squint a bit, that's it, now concentrate on that bit by the serving hatch. See it?

BILL No.

TONY Yes look, it's there, plain as eggs. Look see, there's his nose, that's his pipe, and there's his hat. See it?

BILL No.

TONY (*Gets a bit annoyed*) Of course you can see it. There's dozens of them all over the room. Look, there's Churchill [12] over there, Charlie Chaplin [13] over the mantelpiece, concentrate, squint man, squint … don't shut them … can't you see them?

BILL No.

TONY Oh go and sit down. You wait till you want me to see anything.

HATTIE All I can see on the wallpaper are bunches of grapes.

TONY Who's asking you? Of course you can see bunches

[12] **Churchill** – Sir Winston Churchill, Conservative politician, prime minster and author (1874–1965)
[13] **Charlie Chaplin** – famous film actor, director and scriptwriter who started in silent films (1889–1977)

of grapes, that's the pattern. You've got to use your imagination to see the little faces. (*Pause*) What's the time?

BILL The little hand's on …

TONY Oh not you, somebody else.

HATTIE Seventeen minutes past two.

TONY Seventeen minutes … doesn't time drag? (*Pause*) I can't see that little old man with a pipe now. What angle did I have my head at? Oh yes, there he is. He's got a dog with him now. (*Pause. Sings*) Only a rose I bring you, only a rose to you … (*Pause*)

NEY & TONY (*Together*) Here's a funny thing … I was just thinking …

TONY Pardon?

SIDNEY No, no, after you.

TONY No, no, go on, what were you going to say?

SIDNEY Oh nothing, nothing.

NEY & TONY I was just going to say … I was just going to say …

TONY (*Little laugh*) What were you going to say?

SIDNEY It doesn't matter, nothing important. What were you going to say?

TONY I've forgotten now.

SIDNEY Oh.

TONY (*Sings*) Bom, bom, bom, bom, bom, bom, bom, bom … (*Pause. Changes the tune*) Da, de dum, da de dum de da … what's that called, Sid?

SIDNEY What's what called?

TONY This tune. Da de de dum, da de dum de da.

SIDNEY I don't know.

TONY Don't you remember the film, old Anton Walbrook on the piano?

SIDNEY No.

TONY Oh. (*Pause*) Let's go to the pictures.

HATTIE They don't open till half past four. It's Sunday.

TONY Well, never mind, we'll go at half past four. What's on?

HATTIE Let's see, the Royal Cheam, Bette Davis and George Brent in Little Foxes, and The Battle of Little Bighorn.

TONY Oh. I've seen them. I've seen both of them. It's always the same on Sundays. They always put on old films that you've seen before. Makes you sick. What's on at the other place?

HATTIE It's closed down.

TONY Oh. So much for the pictures. (*Pause*) What time do the pubs open?

SIDNEY Seven o'clock.

TONY Oh cor. Even that's open an hour later than weekdays. And they close earlier. There's no one up there Sunday nights anyway. Except the barmaid. And she's a bit off. I told Harry. I said to him, 'What did you get rid of Gladys for?' She was a fair piece. Her arms were a bit thick, but what can you expect when she's pulling pints all day long? But this one … oh dear, oh dear, puts you right off beer, she does. You want to get it down quickly and get out. I told Harry straight. I said, 'Harry, you've done wrong there, getting rid of Gladys. There's no attraction coming in here now, cos your beer's rotten'.

SIDNEY Did you tell him that?

TONY Certainly. He didn't deny it. It's fallen right off, that place. Well, the dart club's moved down to the Bull.

SIDNEY Why don't he get rid of her then?

TONY I think there's something going on between those two. He had a black eye the other day and he's been drinking more.

SIDNEY Shame. I like Harry.

TONY So do I. But there you are. These women, once they get hold of you, mate, there you are. That's the way it goes.

SIDNEY Yeah.

TONY Yes. That's life. It's always the same. There you are. Up one minute, down the next.

SIDNEY Yeah.

TONY You never know when it's your turn next.

SIDNEY No.

TONY That's the way it goes. You never know what's round the next corner, do you?

SIDNEY True. No matter how bad off you are, there's always somebody worse off than yourself.

TONY That's very true. I was just thinking about poor old Albert in hospital. He's been there a month, and no one's been to see him.

SIDNEY Haven't they really, poor old devil?

TONY No one's been near him. He's just laying there.

SIDNEY Oh dear, makes you feel rotten, don't it?

TONY Poor old Albert.

SIDNEY Well look, why don't we go and see him this afternoon? We haven't got anything to do.

TONY (*Pause*) No, it's a long way, isn't it? He's probably asleep. We'll go next week.

SIDNEY Yeah.

Pause.

Manhattan Transfer

RADIO 4
Word of Mouth
Series 8 Programme 1
TX: 20 August 1996
Presenter: Russell Davies

DAVIES … The Dirty Dozens or more simply the Dozens was an insult game carried on among and between African-Americans … and still practised today under various new names. 'Snapping' is the name favoured in New York and the most fashionable and yet socially responsible Snappers are a trio, called 'Two Brothers and a White Guy', who found a use for this verbal daredevilry that goes beyond mere entertainment. I met the 'White Guy', James Percelay, in Bryant Park in mid-town Manhattan; which was remarkable in itself. A very few years ago, I wouldn't have wanted to meet anybody in Bryant Park, thank you very much, so drug-haunted was the whole place. But several areas of Manhattan have been cleared up and this is one of them. Soon we were joined by one of the 'Brothers', the real inheritors of this tradition, Monteria Ivey.

MONTERIA (*Laughs*) Well, I was hosting a club, the 'Uptown Comedy Club' up in Harlem and one night James decided to be like Columbus and venture up into the New World and came up to Harlem and he happened to be the only white guy sitting in the audience that night …

JAMES … and the host of the show looked at me and started insulting me in a very curious manner and his first insult was: 'You're so white, you think Malcolm X [14] is Malcolm the Tenth.'

MONTERIA   And fortunately our other partner, Stefon, Stefon Douek, happened to be in the crowd that night – he and I grew up together – and he was sitting next to Jim, so he leaned over to him and told him: 'Don't worry about it, we do this all the time'; cos I was snapping on him.

JAMES   And he proceeded with this barrage of insults, which were scary, at the same time entertaining, and after the show the three of us met, because he introduced me to the host of the show.

MONTERIA   And it just seemed logical what the name should be, because it had been two brothers and a white guy.

Rap song
'All right, you know the rules, you can't touch the man, but you can say anything you want about him. You can talk about his family, talk about his friends, talk about his mother, if you have to … and if you don't like it …'

JAMES   Snapping is the African-American art of verbal insults.

DAVIES   Right.

JAMES   Things like: 'If ugliness were bricks, your mother would be a housing project'. That's a snap. (Davies: Right, right.)

---

[14] **Malcolm X** – leader of the Black Muslims; influential in campaigns for racial equality in America (1925–65)

Snaps sketch

JAMES   (*Laughter*) 'Your mother's so old, she did the guest list for Noah's Ark!' (*Laughs*)
'Your mother's so old, when she was a kid, rainbows was black and white.'
(*Laughter*)

MONTERIA   The object of the game is to try and get under the skin of your opponent and to make them lose their cool, because the first person who can't come back verbally and loses their cool is the loser, when you play the game. And it's all done in good humour, I mean, you grow up playing with your friends.

Snaps sketch

'Your father's so dumb, when the judge said "Order in the Court", he said: "I's have fried chicken wings and some fried eggs."' (*Laughter*)

DAVIES   It's a kind of paradox, isn't it? Because it is provoking, it is (Monteria: Oh provoking.) a provocation and yet it's a way of letting provocations not go too far.

MONTERIA   Right. And the reason it's so provoking though for the layman is that so many of the most popular snaps begin with 'Your mother ...' or some other member of your family, but usually your mother is the most popular, okay; so I might talk about somebody's family, like I might mention that James's family was so poor they used to go to Kentucky Fried Chicken to lick other people's fingers, or I might talk about his sister, who was so dumb she once climbed a tree in the hopes of becoming a Branch Manager. (*Both laugh*) Or I might talk about his father, who used to sleep with a ruler beside the bed, so you could see how long he slept; but the most popular ones tend to be where you start talking about 'your mother'.

JAMES   Yeah, and all men share a reverence for the mother, so that was like the big bomb: 'Your mother's so fat, she eats her cereal out of a satellite dish!'

Mother gags
'Your mother's so dumb, she told me to meet her on the corner, Walk and Don't Walk, she'd be standing by the pole.'
'Your mother's so stupid. I said: "What do you think about the Simpson case?" She said: "Now, boy, don't kill those kids."'
'Your mother's so stupid, she snuck on the bus and paid to get off.'

MONTERIA   Like, for instance, 'Gee, your mother's so old, she was a waitress at the Last Supper! "More wine, Jesus?"' (*Laughs*) And the thing is you shouldn't think of it as: 'Oh they're really talking about each other's family members.' No, we're just having fun (Davies: Yeah.) with the language (Davies: Yeah.) and with each other.

Mother gags
'Your mother's so fat, she can't lose weight, she just keeps finding it.' (*Laughter*)

DAVIES   This is obviously a technique where new inventions are the great thing, I mean, thinking up new lines, new ways of doing it. (Monteria: Oh yeah.) On the other hand, it's an old tradition. Aren't there, aren't there sort of set routines of this (Monteria: Right, now ...) that go right back?

MONTERIA   Well, you see, the history of it goes back to slavery. (Davies: Yeah.) and, in fact, in America slaves used to play the game as a means to talk about the Master without the Master being able to figure out what was being said, and originally it had more of a rhyming scheme, where you had to rhyme and be funny, and so the next guy had to not only try to top you, but he had to keep the rhythm going.

JAMES If you plan to be in the snaps battle, don't have a funny haircut. Don't give yourself the opportunity to be picked on. (*Laughs*)

MONTERIA Now folks in Radioland, now you hear Russell, he's got a beautiful speaking voice, but I want you to know that up close and in person, Russell has very hot breath. All right. In fact, his breath is so nasty, he needs a tic tac with a battery. (*Laughter*) No, I'm just kidding. Just kidding. (*Laughter*)

DAVIES Two Brothers and a White Guy snapping for peace, words to make the fighting cease.

Television

'Reading' television, as with many other media, involves 'reading' pictures as well as words and other sounds; and this means not just looking at the subject-matter but at the style of the pictures. This may be fantastic or obviously stylised or it may be made to look realistic. Many of the popular television genres (soap, situation comedy, fly-on-the-wall documentary) work through realism. But this is not the same as the real world as we have come to know it; simply another style, involving as many decisions on what to shoot, how to shoot it and how to edit it as any other style. It is all a matter of selection and construction.

Television has become so much part of everyday life, so much a part of the furniture, that we tend to take it for granted. But its messages are among the most influential in our lives. So, amid the apparent variety, we need to look at patterns in it: patterns in programming (genre, for instance), patterns of representation of different groups (who is shown? how? who is invisible?) and patterns of opinion (whose voice has weight?).

The selection here includes extracts from two comedy shows, two soaps and two hospital programmes – one, a documentary; the other, a drama.

The Dead Parrot

MONTY PYTHON'S FLYING CIRCUS
TX: 7 December 1969

Pet shop. Mr Praline walks into shop carrying a dead parrot in a cage. He walks to counter where shopkeeper tries to hide below cash register.

PRALINE (*John Cleese*)   Hello, I wish to register a complaint … Hello? Miss?

SHOPKEEPER (*Michael Palin*)   What do you mean – Miss?

PRALINE   Oh, I'm sorry, I have a cold. I wish to make a complaint.

SHOPKEEPER   Sorry, we're closing for lunch.

PRALINE   Never mind that my lad. I wish to complain about this parrot what I purchased not half an hour ago from this very boutique.

SHOPKEEPER   Oh yes, the Norwegian Blue. What's wrong with it?

PRALINE   I'll tell you what's wrong with it. It's dead, that's what's wrong with it.

SHOPKEEPER   No, no, it's resting, look!

PRALINE   Look my lad, I know a dead parrot when I see one and I'm looking at one right now.

SHOPKEEPER   No, no sir, it's not dead. It's resting.

PRALINE   Resting?

SHOPKEEPER   Yeah, remarkable bird the Norwegian Blue. Beautiful plumage, innit?

PRALINE   The plumage don't enter into it – it's stone dead.

SHOPKEEPER   No, no – it's just resting.

PRALINE   All right then, if it's resting I'll wake it up. (*Shouts into cage*) Hello Polly! I've got a nice cuttlefish for you when you wake up, Polly Parrot!

SHOPKEEPER (*Jogging cage*) There it moved.

PRALINE No he didn't. That was you pushing the cage.

SHOPKEEPER I did not.

PRALINE Yes, you did. (*Takes parrot out of cage, shouts*) Hello Polly, Polly. (*Bangs it against counter*) Polly Parrot, wake up, Polly. (*Throws it in the air and lets it fall to the floor*) Now that's what I call a dead parrot.

SHOPKEEPER No, no, it's stunned.

PRALINE Look my lad, I've just about had enough of this. That parrot is definitely deceased. And when I bought it not half an hour ago, you assured me that its lack of movement was due to it being tired and shagged out after a long squawk.

SHOPKEEPER It's probably pining for the fiords [15].

PRALINE Pining for the fiords, what kind of talk is that? Look, why did it fall flat on its back the moment I got home?

SHOPKEEPER The Norwegian Blue prefers kipping on its back. Beautiful bird, lovely plumage.

PRALINE Look, I took the liberty of examining that parrot, and I discovered that the only reason that it had been sitting on its perch in the first place was that it had been nailed there.

SHOPKEEPER Well of course it was nailed there. Otherwise it would muscle up to those bars and voom.

PRALINE Look matey, (*Picks up parrot*) this parrot wouldn't voom if I put four thousand volts through it. It's bleeding demised.

SHOPKEEPER It's not, it's pining.

PRALINE It's not pining, it's passed on. This parrot is no more. It has ceased to be. It's expired and gone to meet its maker. This is a late parrot. It's a stiff.

---

[15] **fiords** – narrow sea inlets between mountains

Bereft of life, it rests in peace. If you hadn't nailed it to the perch, it would be pushing up the daisies. It's rung down the curtain and joined the choir invisible. This is an ex-parrot.

SHOPKEEPER   Well, I'd better replace it then.

PRALINE   (*To camera*) If you want to get anything done in this country, you've got to complain till you're blue in the mouth.

SHOPKEEPER   Sorry guv, we're right out of parrots.

PRALINE   I see. I see. I get the picture.

SHOPKEEPER   I've got a slug.

PRALINE   Does it talk?

SHOPKEEPER   Not really, no.

PRALINE   Well, it's scarcely a replacement then, is it?

SHOPKEEPER   Listen, I'll tell you what, (*Handing over a card*) tell you what. If you go to my brother's shop in Bolton he'll replace your parrot for you.

PRALINE   Bolton eh?

SHOPKEEPER   Yeah.

PRALINE   All right.

He leaves, holding the parrot.

CAPTION: 'A SIMILAR PET SHOP IN BOLTON, LANCS'

Close-up of sign on door reading: 'Similar Pet Shops Ltd'. Pull back from sign to see same pet shop. Shopkeeper now has moustache. PRALINE walks into shop. He looks around with interest, noticing the empty parrot cage still on the floor.

PRALINE   Er, excuse me. This is Bolton, is it?

SHOPKEEPER   No, no, it's, er, Ipswich.

PRALINE   (*To camera*) That's Inter-City Rail for you. (*Leaves*)

Man in porter's outfit standing at complaints desk for railways. PRALINE approaches.

PRALINE   I wish to make a complaint.

PORTER   (*Terry Jones*)   I don't have to do this, you know.

PRALINE   I beg your pardon?

PORTER   I'm a qualified brain surgeon. I only do this because I like being my own boss.

PRALINE   Er, excuse me, this is irrelevant, isn't it?

PORTER   Oh yeah, it's not easy to pad these out to thirty minutes.

PRALINE   Well I wish to make a complaint. I got on the Bolton train and found myself deposited here in Ipswich.

PORTER   No, this is Bolton.

PRALINE   (*To camera*) The pet shop owner's brother was lying.

PORTER   Well you can't blame British Rail for that.

PRALINE   If this is Bolton, I shall return to the pet shop.

CAPTION: 'A LITTLE LATER LTD'

Praline walks into the shop again.

PRALINE   I understand that this is Bolton.

SHOPKEEPER   Yes.

PRALINE   Well, you told me it was Ipswich.

SHOPKEEPER   It was a pun.

PRALINE   A pun?

SHOPKEEPER   No, no, not a pun, no. What's the other thing which reads the same backwards as forwards?

PRALINE   A palindrome?

SHOPKEEPER   Yes, yes.

PRALINE   It's not a palindrome. The palindrome of Bolton would be Notlob. It don't work.

SHOPKEEPER   Look, what do you want?

PRALINE   No, I'm sorry, I'm not prepared to pursue my line of enquiry any further as I think this is getting too silly.

Fashion

ABSOLUTELY FABULOUS
by Jennifer Saunders
TX: 12 November 1992

Scene 5 Edina's Kitchen

SAFFRON *is sitting at the table reading a newspaper. In front of her are the empty wine bottles and left-over take-aways from Edina and Patsy's binge the night before.* EDINA *enters struggling to appear bright, alive and healthy.* SAFFRON *watches her icily.* EDINA *removes her tinted contact lenses, and it is obvious she cannot see a thing.*

EDINA (*Humming to herself*) La, la la, la-la-la. (*She goes to fridge and gets bottle of Evian. She swigs it back and it suctions onto her face. She painfully pulls it off.*) Health, health, health.

She breezes round the kitchen opening cupboards and looking for something for breakfast. She opens the dishwasher, then the washing machine.

SAFFRON Washing machine.

EDINA La-la, la-la! Absolutely right, sweetie. (*Opens freezer door*) Just checking the contents. La, la, la. (*She does manic deep-breathing whilst slapping ice-cubes on her face.*)

SAFFRON (*Tapping the wine bottles pointedly with a pen*) Feeling great, I expect, this morning, are you?

EDINA (*Slamming freezer door*) Fabulous. My god ... Patsy can put it away. (*She gives up looking for something to eat and staggers into a chair.*) Stop looking at me like that. What do I have to do to convince you that I've given up drinking? (*Pauses*) I had one drink. I mean, for god's sake, are you accusing me?

SAFFRON Have you looked in the mirror this morning? Your eyebags are ruched. [16]

EDINA What are you eating?

SAFFRON Toast.

EDINA What is that on the toast?

SAFFRON It's honey, mother.

EDINA Oh, my god … Oh, my god. Honey! That's not honey. Sweetie, that's my bloody royal jelly moisturiser. You are eating £300-worth of royal jelly that has been hand-squished from a bee's backside. And not just any old bee, but the bloody Gucci of bees. This is the stuff that Jackie Stallone would kill for. (EDINA *scrapes it off the toast and rubs it onto her face.*) That's better. (*To* SAFFRON) Make me a cup of tea, darling. I've got a dreadful day ahead.

SAFFRON You know where it is – make it yourself.

EDINA I don't know where it bloody is, do I?

SAFFRON Please don't swear.

EDINA Sweetie … darling, please fetch mama a cup of coffee. You're so clever, darling, you know where everything is, sweetie. I think it's so clever to know exactly where things are. I do think you're marvellous …

SAFFRON Flattery won't turn me into your servant. The coffee is on the table in front of you … Pick up a spoon … Put coffee in cup … Pour on boiling water.

EDINA Scald hand … Third-degree burns … Screaming in agony. Do you really want that on your conscience, darling?

SAFFRON All right. (*She gets up to make the coffee.*)

---

[16] **ruched** – pleated

EDINA Not instant, darling. Grind some beans. That's not proper coffee ... that's just beans that have been cremated. I want them entire with lifeforce.

SAFFRON *puts beans in the grinder.*

EDINA And don't make that face when you grind. I don't want to drink a cup full of your anger. Anyway, I shouldn't be drinking coffee ... throw it all away. Throw all the coffee away. I don't want coffee. I just want some fennel ... twig ... tea.

SAFFRON *sits down.*

EDINA Oh, god, look at the time. (*Grabbing the telephone she rings the office. Then she grabs* SAFFRON *and puts the phone to her ear.*) Sweetie, tell them I've left. Tell them it's traffic door-to-door, and I'm not well.

SAFFRON Hallo ... my mother's sitting here in her dressing-gown ...

EDINA (*Grabs the phone, furious*) Dressing-gown! Ha! Ha! She knows nothing about fashion. Now, Bubble, darling, I'm in a dreadful panic. I'm literally out the door when my bloody car turns up. I understand the traffic's awful. I'm desperately trying to keep a lid on things this end and I know you can manage that end. I'm frantic. I'm on my way ... chanting as we speak. Bye. (*She puts down phone.* SAFFRON *smirks.* EDINA *notices.*) Oh ... ha-ha! You're not a Buddhist ... you wouldn't understand.

SAFFRON Mum, you did it for a week. Which, admittedly for you, is a record.

EDINA Darling, it's not a fad. It's not like crystals. (*She starts a chant, but can't remember it.*)

SAFFRON Please stop.

EDINA You wouldn't say that if you knew how much we

68

owed to my chanting. A lot of things in this house wouldn't be here … This house wouldn't be here … I chanted for this gorgeous house. I chanted to be successful, to believe in myself. (*Chants*) Please let me make some more money so that I can buy Saffron some more books and a car. (*Pause*) In Buddhist, obviously … not in English when I do it properly.

SAFFRON What is it … some sort of cosmic cash machine?

EDINA Don't be cynical. Not today. Today I need a little support.

SAFFRON Why is today such a panic anyway? It's only a fashion show and you've had six months to prepare it. Why is everything always so hysterical? All you've got to do is play a bit of music, turn on the lights, get some people who've thrown up everything they've ever eaten and send them down a catwalk. Greater feats have been achieved in less time and with less fuss.

EDINA You're not quite with it, are you, darling?

SAFFRON Major motion pictures are made, huge concerts are put on in stadiums, for god's sake. Five-hundred thousand troops were mobilised in the Gulf and a war fought and won in less time, and without everyone involved having a nervous breakdown and being sent flowers. It cannot be that difficult.

EDINA But, darling, every troop didn't have to contain Yasmin Le Bon. The generals didn't require big hugs after every manoeuvre. And the whole operation didn't have to be coordinated to rap and Japanese avant garde pipe music. Because I think, if it had, the outcome might have been very different. Now if you'll excuse me, I'm going to get dressed. (*She gets up, then sits down again, picks up the phone and dials*) I forgot to ring Chukhani. He was going to channel a colour for me to wear today. Hallo, Chukhani? (*Pause*) Edina … (*Pauses again*) Green … Thank you. (*Puts the phone down*) Don't look at me like that, Saffy darling. There is more to it.

SAFFRON Of course, there is. The bill.

EDINA He doesn't pick any colour himself. It is channelled to him by an ancient spirit who understands perfectly my karma and relates it to who I was in a previous existence.

SAFFRON So, who were you then in your previous life? I suppose the Elizabeth Taylor of the Ming Dynasty. Face up to it – you're just a mad, fat, old cow.

EDINA (*Gets up in rage*)Will you stop saying 'fat'. I know you're only saying it to annoy me. Stop it! Stop it!

SAFFRON I'm saying it because it's true.

JIMMY'S

Series 12 Programme 5

V/O   At Europe's largest teaching hospital, St James's in Leeds, the stories continue. Today, Reg Knee will find out if the suspicious growth removed from his bowel was a cancerous tumour. One week after the surgery on his perforated eardrum, Ben Fielding returns to Out-Patients for a check-up. Ten-year-old Jamie Cornthwaite arrives in theatre for an operation to stop his curved spine deforming any further. Harry Swallow is getting ready to go home two weeks after his hip-replacement operation. And Laura Morton has chronic liver disease. She's come to hospital for tests, to find out if she's fit enough for a life-saving liver transplant.

DOCTOR   What took you to your GP ... in the first place?

LAURA   The itching ... skin badly itching.

DOCTOR   So that's been going for ... ?

LAURA   Eight years over.

DOCTOR   Eight years. And that was the first symptom?

LAURA   That was the first symptom I got.

DOCTOR   OK. We know that you've got this diagnosis of primary biliary cirrhosis, or PBC for short. That is a chronic condition. It's not a condition which tends to get better. Once you've got it, it tends to be fairly progressive. You've tried all the medications that we've got. They haven't worked. So really we're now down to looking at a liver transplant. Obviously

71

that's a big operation, it's a major undertaking, and therefore we've got to make sure you're fit enough to go through that. So, whilst you're here we've got various investigations we need to do. The first of these, later on today, will be an ultrasound scan, looking at the texture of the liver and what the blood vessels are like, but we'll also be concentrating on the heart and lungs, not because they're involved in this condition, but, if you're going to go through a big operation, then it's going to put a lot of stress on the heart and lungs, so we've got to be sure in a lady of 64 that's up to it. And once we've got all the information together, then we'll come back and have a chat with you and give you a realistic opinion as to what we can do.

LAURA   Thank you very much.

CU sign: ANAESTHETIC IN PROGRESS

NURSE   Let's get you up better. That's better. May I beat you up a little bit? (*Tapping* JAMIE*'s hand*)

DOCTOR   That's it, that's it. Just let it go loose and flap now.

MOTHER   So brave.

DOCTOR   And what've you got to do with your toes?

JAMIE   Have to wriggle them.

DOCTOR   Wriggle them. That's it ... a tiny bit of these and I want you to wriggle your toes for me. All right. Can you wriggle them? That's it.

NURSE   Very good.

DOCTOR   Would you let me know when you start to feel a bit sleepy? Right.

MOTHER   See you later. OK, James?

JAMES   See you.

MOTHER   See you, love.

NURSE   Give him a quick kiss?

MOTHER OK? (*Kisses James*) He's gone, hasn't he? Right? Bye.
JAMES Bye.

CU sign: WARD 23

NURSE I just want to have a look to see how your hip's moving. I just want a little check with your walking.
HARRY Yes, yes. Look, I kept my slipper on. (*Tapping foot with metal crutch*)
NURSE It's good to see you're showing your independence.
HARRY I can't get a hammer, otherwise I'd do it with a hammer. I'll tell you what I do now. I get this leg on the bed and I grab this. (*Reaching up to bar above bed*)
NURSE Can you do it without grabbing on to that though, as you won't have one at home.
NURSE 2 You won't have one of those things at home, Harry. That's what we're trying to get things sorted out, so that you're all ready and set.
HARRY I ought to get the joinery set out and make a frame.
NURSE What you need to do is try and slide your legs, little by little, to the very edge and then you want to use your arms to push yourself forward and up. That's it. And then bring your other leg. That's it. Perfect.
NURSE 2 Ah, you've got it mastered.
HARRY Didn't use the bar then, eh?
NURSE 2 Well done. That's it, you see. Now hang on.
NURSE Now, you should remember when you're standing you should stand with your crutches in one hand …
HARRY Whilst … when I'm standing?
NURSE Yes. I'll show … now you're stood, we'll have a little walk, but I'll show you when we get back.
HARRY Yes, yes.
NURSE 2 Remember, you're pushing all your weight through that leg.

HARRY I haven't got a right lot of pain, you know.
NURSE 2 Good.

CU sign: EAR, NOSE AND THROAT CLINICS

DOCTOR I'm just gonna have a look now, Ben. It's a little bit cold this. OK? Oh, that looks absolutely super. It all looks to be healing up nicely. Okey doke. (*To Ben's mother*) When I put the dressing in the ear for the start of the operation, I put a dissolving dressing in as well.

MOTHER Yes.

DOCTOR That'll slowly come out over the next couple of weeks. What I'm going to do is give you some drops to use for the next two weeks and then I'll see him back in about a month, and by then the ear should be dry and settled down. It all looks absolutely super. It's all healing up nicely.

BEN Will I be able to hear properly now?

DOCTOR Yes. I mean, it'll take a little while because you've still got some dressing inside there that'll dissolve away. But by the time I next see you it should be a lot better and what we'll do at that stage is get a hearing test, to see what your hearing's like, and then you'll be able to go swimming.

Ben grins.

Ward 23

NURSE Make sure you can feel the chair behind you and before you sit down pop your crutches off. That's it.

HARRY Put them together?

NURSE Yes. Hold in one hand and then reach for the chair with the other and then slide that leg out. That's it. That's lovely.

NURSE 2   Well done … sack of potatoes.

NURSE   A little bit of a dive down. Well done.

HARRY   I nearly made a mess of everything, Alison. You know I like that 'Fifteen to One' programme, see. So I thought I'll watch it with that chap over there, the footballer with a broken leg, so I said 'I'll come with you' and without thinking I went into the day-room and I sat on one of those plastic chairs.

NURSE 2   Don't tell Mr MacDonald that.

HARRY   And when the programme was over, I couldn't get up, and when I thought about it afterwards, I thought 'You idiot'. Anyway, I think my wife is the sort of person who'll put a curb on me.

NURSE   Good. That's what we're here for. (*Laughs*)

HARRY   She's a bit strict in that sense.

NURSE 2   She'll tell you who's boss, I'm sure, Harry.

NURSE   We're good at nagging.

HARRY   Sometimes I think she's nagging me, but she has a good heart you know. I'm sure it's all to my good.

NURSE 2   You'll be looking forward to getting home then, eh?

HARRY   I am.

NURSE 2   I thought you would.

CU sign: THEATRES

Operation on BEN. *His back has been opened up and the surgeon is making holes in the bones of his back.*

SURGEON   That's sort of … spine … nice controlled test with this … What we're doing now is making good solid hook sites, so we don't have any mechanical failure and the hooks don't dislodge or get out because they haven't been properly inserted. And this is the lower hook site as you can see … That's a beautiful hook site there. And what is at the bottom of that is

the lining of the spinal cord, the dura, down there
… Now let's have the hook, please. That's it. That's
it there. Rod, please. Bender, please, David…
(*Finding the equipment hard to undo*) … the damn
thing! … (*Inserts metal alongside James's spine*) …
Quite frankly, it should work OK.

Another room

DOCTOR We now have the histology from the specimen that
we removed, and that's clearly what you've been
waiting for us to talk to you about. If I tell you that,
as far as the histologist is concerned, there's no
suspicion that there's tumour left behind. That's
the most important thing about it, as far as we can
tell. But there are some features within the area of
the bowel that he's looked at under the microscope
that suggest you might benefit from some more
treatment. Now this 'more treatment' is going to be
drugs, chemotherapy, if that is what you chose to
have. Our worry is clearly that, if you do not have
the treatment, then there is a possibility that it will
come back.

REG Really? Um.

DOCTOR Now, the purpose of the treatment is to clear up any
little cells that we cannot see and the pathologist
can't see that may be lurking around the area we've
been operating in.

REG I must confess that it's taken the wind out of my
sails a bit, you know. It's gone and taken away and
… you know … end-of-story kind of thing.

DOCTOR Um, well, would that that were the case in every
single situation, but in our experience there are
times when it's not the case.

Value For Money

CASUALTY
Series 8 Episode 18
by Allan Swift

Characters

Regulars

CHARLIE FAIRHEAD, Clinical Nurse Manager

DOCTOR MIKE BARRATT, Casualty Consultant

DAVE MASTERS, Senior House Officer

NURSE MARTIN ASHFORD (ASH), Senior Staff Nurse

ADELE BECKFORD, staff nurse

RACHEL LONGWORTH, staff nurse

MARY SKILLETT, staff nurse

MIE NISHI-KAWA, receptionist

JANE SCOTT, A & E Manager

JOSH GRIFFITHS, paramedic

BRIAN CRAWFORD, ambulance technician

FRANKIE DRUMMER, porter

Non regulars

TED DANIELS

MRS DANIELS, Ted's wife

TREVOR, football coach

PAUL BECKETT, circulation problem

ANNA BECKETT, Paul's wife

PETER BECKETT, their son

1 EXT. CAR PARK. DAY. 13.35

CHARLIE *heading for A & E, turns on hearing:*

MARY   Charlie! (*She catches up with him, they keep walking*) Can I ask you something?

CHARLIE   Ten minutes before the shift starts.

MARY   I'm worried ... (*He waits*) ... about my job – holding onto it, I mean.

CHARLIE   (*Nods*) There's a lot of it about.

MARY   What are my chances?

CHARLIE   (*Shrugs*) There could be some highly qualified people looking for jobs if Queens closes. But ... there is something you could do.

He walks on. MARY *runs to catch up.*

MARY   What's that?

CHARLIE   Make yourself indispensable.

Walks on again.

MARY   I thought I was! (*She runs to catch up*) Charlie!

2 INT. RECEPTION. DAY. 13.47

ASH *approaches desk and plonks a Tupperware lunch box onto the desk as* FRANKIE *ambles past.*

MIE   If that's ticking I'm calling security.

ASH   (*Proud*) This, is a genuine Japanese dish – Teriyaki, no less – made by my own fair hands. (*Opens lid*)

FRANKIE   (*Interested*) I'm into oriental food.

ASH   Then try the Chinese takeaway.

FRANKIE   The Chinese doing Japanese food now? – that Common Market's got a lot to answer for.

As FRANKIE *ambles away, see* CHARLIE *and* MARY *enter;* CHARLIE *notes* ASH, *still in civvies.*

CHARLIE How come everybody's early?

MARY Scared for their job?

3 EXT. AMBULANCE/STREET. DAY 13.50

Int. ambulance: JOSH *at the wheel,* BRIAN *and a distraught* MRS DANIELS *sitting by her husband who is sitting at forty-five degrees on the stretcher.* BRIAN *checks the oxygen mask on* MR DANIELS, *wires him up to the cardiac monitor, takes his BP.*

JOSH Don't worry, love, we'll soon have him there.

RS DANIELS (*Near to tears*) … we don't have any money left.

BRIAN How old is he, Mrs Daniels?

MR DANIELS *groans.*

RS DANIELS Seventy-one, he'll be at the back of the queue, won't he?

JOSH He'll be seen the minute we get him to Holby, love, don't you worry.

RS DANIELS We used up all our savings you see.

BRIAN Just try and keep calm, eh?

He places her hand in MR DANIELS'.

RS DANIELS (*Quiet*) I knew this would happen again.

BRIAN Again?

4 INT. STAFF ROOM. DAY. 13.55

MARY *fills kettle.* RACHEL *sits reading a magazine.* ASH *has his white coat on and is peering into fridge.*

MARY What d'you think, Ash?

ASH About what?

MARY What's the matter with you people? This is important. Are we hired or fired? Well what do you think?

ASH   I think … yes. I think we need a bigger fridge.

See MARY *glumly frustrated.* RACHEL *looks up from her magazine.*

RACHEL   It's a survival of the most qualified. And why not?

ASH *stands, closes fridge door, looks at* RACHEL, *then at* MARY.

ASH   I don't want to speculate. I want facts.

5 *EXT. FOOTBALL PITCH. DAY. 13.57*

A keenly fought amateur football match in progress; from front seat of car some fifteen yards from the pitch PAUL, *pulling on a cigarette, watches his enthusiastic wife,* ANNA, *cheer on their son,* PETER. *Pacing nervously along the touchline* TREVOR, *the team's vociferous trainer/coach.*

TREVOR   Get a grip, ref. Protect the ball, players!

ANNA   Come on, Peter … !

TREVOR   C'mon now, United, they're panicking, that's why they're fouling, they don't know what else to do!!

PAUL *flicks the cigarette butt out of the window. Follows the game with a shrewd, almost professional, interest.*

TREV. & ANNA   (*Together*) Corner!?

TREVOR   Oh ref-er-ree – use your eyes – that was a corner!

PAUL *notices* TREVOR *offer cigarette to* ANNA *who accepts.*

ANNA   Come on, Peter … !

TREVOR *then follows the play down the touchline.*

TREVOR   Now face up, United, hold the line, that's it – push up, push up back four, that's it, that's it … !

PETER *is chopped down by one of the opposing players.*

See PAUL *in the car mouth angrily 'Foul'. Show* ANNA
protesting vehemently with TREVOR *who's running onto
the pitch to attend the nearby* PETER. ANNA *runs over to be
as near as she can.*

ANNA   Foul, ref!!

TREVOR   That's the fourth time he's done that, ref!

ANNA   That's a terrible foul.

TREVOR*'s now crouching down, attending to* PETER, *who is
writhing in pain, clutching his thigh.* PAUL *gets out of his
car. He winces with pain and limps over to the barrier.*

6 INT. STAFF COFFEE ROOM. DAY. 14.00

Reasonably peopled, including DAVE, ASH, RACHEL *and*
MARY.

ASH   Common policy: keep Frankie away from the fridge.
OK … ?

But before there's a response, CHARLIE *enters.*

CHARLIE   Right. The shift starts here. A shocked MI in about
eight minutes … seventy-one years old.

7 EXT. FOOTBALL PITCH. DAY. 14.01

The match continues in background. ANNA *walks with*
TREVOR *and* PETER *towards the car (and therefore* PAUL)
during:

PETER   I'm alright, Trevor – honest.

TREVOR   It's just a precaution. I'm not taking any chances
with the cup tie next week.

PAUL   Give him some support, will you? – take the strain
off his ankle.

TREVOR   Oh right, yeh.

PETER It's just a bruise, dad, I'll be okay.

ANNA May as well do this properly … (*Discards cigarette, entwines* PETER*'s other arm around her shoulder*) Trevor. (*Offers her hand to him*)

TREVOR Got you, right.

HE *and* ANNA *make a 'chair' with their hands for* PETER.

PETER I can walk, y' know.

ANNA Shall we drop him then, Trev?

PAUL *watches* TREVOR *share the laugh with* ANNA *as they carry* PETER *towards the car. He pulls on his cigarette.*

8 EXT. OUTSIDE CASUALTY. DAY. 14.10

Ambulance doors open to ASH *and* CHARLIE. *They wheel* MR DANIELS *into the hospital.*

BRIAN This is Mr Daniels; collapsed with chest pain.

JOSH He had an MI two months ago.

BRIAN BP of 70/40, we've given him ten milligrams of nubane and oxygen.

MRS DANIELS (*Terrified*) Please help him. We haven't got any money left.

BRIAN He was probably given streptokinase then.

ASH Thank you for that, Doctor.

JOSH Brian … (*Lay off, OK?*)

CHARLIE Can you hear me, Mr Daniels?

9 INT. ANNA AND PAUL'S HOUSE. FRONT ROOM. DAY. 14.45

PAUL *on sofa with foot up, reading a newspaper and trying to ignore the conversation and laughter coming from the connecting room.*

10 INT. ANNA AND PAUL'S HOUSE. BACK ROOM. DAY

PETER *still in football kit.* ANNA *and* TREVOR *talk quietly.* TREVOR *takes the cigarette* ANNA *offers.*

TREVOR I'm definitely giving this up next birthday.

ANNA Paul and me too.

PETER Same old story, same old song.

TREVOR How's Gazza?

PETER Me crucial ligaments are fine, thanks, 'Graham'.
(*Then, serious, rubs thigh*) It's just a bit tight, that's all.

TREVOR We need you fully fit for next week.

He massages PETER*'s thigh.*

PETER I'll be there, no sweat.
(*Beat*)

TREVOR How're things?

ANNA I'm still having an affair with you.

TREVOR Am I any good?

PETER Oh lay off, you two. (*Pause*) Let's have some tea, eh?

ANNA Okay.

She gets up to go into the kitchen to make tea.

11 INT. TEABAR. DAY. 14.50

JOSH *and* BRIAN *at tea/coffee machine*

JOSH What's with you? (BRIAN *looks*) What's all this 'He would have been given this medication or that' …!

BRIAN I did three years at medical school – I'm up to here with being looked on as a glorified stretcher bearer.

JOSH I did three and a half years to become a paramedic and I don't notice anyone looking down on me … If you feel undervalued, have the guts to go'n finish what you started.

He goes. Stay on BRIAN, *miffed – maybe even defiant/determined.*

12 INT. CUBICLE. DAY. 14.53

MIKE, MARY *and* ASH *in attendance*

MRS DANIELS   We went to Downside – got seen straight away because we paid for it.

ASH   You've paid for this hospital too, Mrs Daniels, and we're seeing to him now.

MIKE   Where's the pain, Mr Daniels? Can you point it out for me, please?

MR DANIELS *groans, gestures re: chest.*

Can you describe the pain?

Just a groan in reply.

Does it feel as though there's a weight pressing down on you here? And down your arm?

MR DANIELS *groans affirmatively to all three questions.* MIKE *turns.*

I want a twelve lead ECG – it looks like an MI but I want to be sure.

Another groan from MR DANIELS.

When you were in Downside, can you remember what drugs you were given, Mr Daniels?

MR DANIELS *groans in pain.*

D'you know what drugs he was given, Mrs Daniels?

MRS DANIELS   Drugs? I don't know …

MIKE   Mr Daniels?

84

MR DANIELS *groans affirmatively.*

In Downside – were you put on a drip, a polythene bag with solution in it, being fed into the back of your hand by a needle?

MR DANIELS *groans.*

(*Turns*) Mrs Daniels, was he given a drip?

.S DANIELS Yes, yes he was.

DANIELS (*Groans*) No …

.S DANIELS No, he wasn't.

DANIELS Painkillers!

.S DANIELS Yes, yes – painkillers We paid for them … I remember.

MIKE (*Looking up*) Charlie …

CHARLIE Yeh, OK.

13 INT. ANNA AND PAUL'S HOUSE. KITCHEN. DAY. 14.55

ANNA *making tea, with* TREVOR. *Out of view scream.*

14 INT. ANNA AND PAUL'S HOUSE. SITTING-ROOM. DAY

PAUL *screaming in agony.* ANNA *and* TREVOR *in.* PETER *hovers in the doorway, watching helplessly.*

PAUL Ahhh … !

ANNA Get a warm towel, Peter – in the airing cupboard.

PAUL Quickly.

ANNA *has rolled up* PAUL*'s trouser leg and is rubbing it furiously.*

He usually leaves it till three in the morning before he kicks off.

PAUL Stop fussing!

PAUL is trying to focus on TREVOR.

ANNA Haven't you got a home to go to?

ANNA Someone told him I was throwing an orgy.

TREVOR You okay, mate?

TREVOR moves over to PAUL, *who is in agony but still able to think.*

PAUL What's it look like? Sod off. <u>She</u> may like you touching her but I don't.

PETER returns with warm towel, tosses it to ANNA.

ANNA (*To* TREVOR) What d'you think?

PAUL I don't need his opinion! Army PE instructor, me. Twenty years in schools. Tough schools an' all. Nothing he can teach me.

ANNA Stop, just stop, Paul. I've had this for eight months, I'm fed up with it! Trevor! Just feel this ankle for me.

And her tone is such that neither TREVOR *nor* PAUL *will gainsay her.* TREVOR *sits down by* PAUL. *He feels* PAUL's *ankle and is surprised.*

PAUL Never seen a torn muscle before?

TREVOR It's really cold.

TREVOR, quite stunned, leaves ANNA *to wrap the towel around* PAUL's *ankle.*

PAUL Put the bloody towel around it.

PETER Torn muscles don't wake you in the middle of the night, dad.

ANNA grabs her coat.

ANNA Enough's enough. Let's go.

PAUL   Go where?

15 INT. CHARLIE'S OFFICE. DAY. 15.00

CHARLIE *waiting on the phone as* MIKE *walks in.*

CHARLIE   They can't find Mr Daniels' records at Downside.
The doctor who treated him is away for the
weekend and their computer is on the blink.

MIKE   GP … ?

CHARLIE *gestures – that's who he's talking to now.*

CHARLIE   Doctor Baldwin – he diagnosed cholesystitis … (*To
telephone*) Ah, yes … right, thank you, Doctor …
sorry to trouble you, bye. (*Replaces receiver*) He
hasn't received any notes from Downside.

MIKE   After two months?!

CHARLIE   Hot news, Mike – all's not as it should be in the
private sector. What's up?

MIKE   He should be given streptokinase – but if he was
given it only a month ago, he'll have an allergic
reaction to it.

He heads for Crash.

16 INT. CUBICLE (CONTINUOUS)

MR DANIELS *is hooked up to ECG.* ASH *checks the reading.*
MRS DANIELS *holding her husband's hand.*

ASH   You can stop worrying, Mr Daniels, you're in good
hands – just try and relax, alright?

MIKE   (*Approaching*) Mr Daniels.

DANIELS   Yes …

MIKE   You're absolutely certain you weren't put on a drip
in Downside?

DANIELS Yeh …

MIKE Good. Then –

MRS DANIELS He might have been.

MIKE What – (*Points*) like this?

MRS DANIELS I can't remember.

MIKE *glances at ECG.*

MIKE Mr Daniels, I'm sorry to keep asking you this but it's very important: at Downside you were only given painkillers, you were not put on a drip – is that correct?

MR DANIELS *affirms.*

MRS DANIELS Why don't you ask them? Get me a phone, I'll do it!

MIKE (*Restraining her*) We have phoned – they can't find his notes.

MRS DANIELS But you have to know – how can you treat him? (*Bewildered*) You must know before you can treat him …

MIKE It would be helpful but it's not a huge problem.

He exchanges a brief look with ASH.

One point five million units of streptokinase.

The Barlows

CORONATION STREET
Episode 1 by Tony Warren
TX: 9 December 1960

The Barlows' living room

In shape the living room is an exact replica of the
Tanner's [17], but it is better furnished and altogether tidier.
A table under the window is set for a meal and the family
are eating. Ida Barlow is a kindly woman somewhere in her
late forties. Her husband Frank is a little older. Once he
might have been muscular but has now gone to seed.

Their son Kenneth is twenty. He has little or no northern
accent and looks faintly out of place in these surroundings.

IDA   Sauce, Kenneth?

KENNETH   No thank you.

IDA   Oh, and I got it specially. You always loved it when
you were little.

KENNETH   Did I?

FRANK *helps himself liberally to the bottled sauce.* KENNETH
*watches and shudders involuntarily. His father looks up
and catches his eye.*

FRANK   What's up?

KENNETH   (*Looking away*) Nothing.

FRANK   What's that snooty expression for then?

---

[17] The Tanners' living room: a door leads on to a corridor. Another
door to the scullery. A window looks out on to the yard and backs of
other gloomy houses. The room is dominated by a black-leaded grate.

KENNETH What snooty expression?

IDA (*Hastily to* KENNETH) That new pullover's turned out a treat. I'll never knit another one in that colour though. Navy blue plays devil with my eyes.

FRANK *again picks up the sauce bottle and helps himself to more.*

KENNETH (*Thinks aloud*) Oh no.

FRANK Don't they do this at college then? I'll bet they don't eat in their shirt-sleeves either.

KENNETH What d'you mean?

FRANK I've been noticin' you lookin' at me.

KENNETH I don't know what you're talking about.

FRANK Oh yes you do. (*With grim satisfaction*) We're not good enough for you.

KENNETH (*Flaring and appealing to his mother*) I never said a word and he starts.

IDA Look, Dad, let's just 'ave one meal in peace for a change.

FRANK Now you know 'e doesn't like to 'ear you call me 'Dad', it's common.

IDA Oh, give over the pair of you. My back's at it again somethin' awful.

FRANK That's what comes of doin' that rotten job. I bet you don't tell your 'igh and mighty friends that, Kenneth.

KENNETH What?

FRANK That your Mother works.

KENNETH It's no secret. She works in a hotel kitchen. If anyone asked me, of course I'd tell them.

IDA (*Sharply*) I don't know what's got into you, Frank. You're edgy enough for six. What's up with you?

FRANK Blame me, I would, it's 'im. (*With gloomy menace*) 'Why do we 'ave to 'ave the bread ready buttered?'

IDA Eh?

FRANK 'E said that yesterday. An' then again tonight. 'Why do we 'ave to 'ave cups of tea with the food?' Well I'll tell you why – I like food swilled down properly, that's why. You want to watch out, Ida, or 'e'll be 'avin' you changin' into an evenin' gown to eat your meals.

This idea pleases FRANK *who shuts up and chomps happily.*

IDA Just look at the clock. Wherever can David 'ave got to? (*To* KENNETH) Did you go into town this afternoon?

KENNETH Yes. Oh, I got a record.

IDA One I'll like?

KENNETH You might. I'm not sure.

IDA Well, you know me. I've always been one for a bit o' good music. We'll put it on when we've washed up and your Dad's 'ad his sleep. If David doesn't hurry up, that chop'll 'ave gone bone-dry in the oven.

KENNETH (*Slightly hesitantly*) Oh, by the way, I'm going out later on.

IDA (*Hesitantly*) Are you meeting a girl?

KENNETH Yes.

IDA Oh.

Pause

KENNETH It's just a girl who's in my year.

IDA The one you got the letter from this morning? Does she come from round 'ere?

KENNETH Not far away. The other side of town.

IDA Are you goin' to their 'ouse then?

KENNETH No. Just into town.

IDA Whereabouts are you meetin' 'er?

KENNETH (*After a moment's hesitation*) The Imperial.

FRANK (*He can't believe his ears*) Where?

91

KENNETH The Imperial Hotel.

FRANK Now listen, Squire, you'd best make your mind up to it because you're not goin' throwin' money away in no Imperial Hotels.

KENNETH (*Faintly mockingly*) What d'you mean 'No Imperial Hotels'?

FRANK I mean what I say an' don't come correctin' me.

KENNETH Look, I'm not asking for any money.

FRANK Oh yes, you've got the money. But where did it come from?

IDA (*Wearily*) Frank. Do we 'ave to go through all this?

FRANK Listen, Ida, I'm not 'avin' you workin' in them stinkin' kitchens at the Imperial for 'im to go chuckin' money back at the place as if it grew on trees. It's downright wicked, that's what it is.

IDA 'E's not goin' spendin' much. Are you love?

FRANK You'd best make up your mind to it, Ken … you're not goin' at all.

DAVID BARLOW *enters from the scullery. He is an eighteen-year-old engineering apprentice, bright, cheerful and thoroughly likeable. He is dressed in a donkey jacket, jeans tucked into his socks and heavy shoes. A canvas lunchbag is slung over one shoulder.*

DAVID Hellow.

IDA An' what time d'you call this?

DAVID I 'ad another puncture.

FRANK (*Mock wearily*) Which one this time?

DAVID Front. I thought it was just the valve at first.

FRANK The sooner you get shot of that ruin, the better. The thing's only fit for t'scrap yard.

DAVID Don't worry. That's just where it's goin' minute I've got enough for the deposit.

IDA Deposit? What on?

DAVID (*Calmly*) What do you think on? A motor bike o' course.

IDA Over my dead body.

IDA *goes into the scullery.*

FRANK Is it rainin'?

DAVID It was a minute or two ago. It's just stopped.

FRANK I'll go out an' 'ave a look at that bike.

DAVID It's alright, Dad. I'll see to it after.

FRANK Where's the puncture outfit?

DAVID In the saddlebag. I've told you though, don't bother about it.

FRANK *picks up a torch and exits through the scullery.*

DAVID (*To* KENNETH) 'ow're you?

KENNETH Alright.

IDA*'s head appears round the scullery door.*

IDA (*Grimly to* DAVID) Do you want gravy?

DAVID Wouldn't mind.

IDA You'll 'ave to wait while I've warmed it up then.

The head disappears.

DAVID Somethin' up, Ken?

KENNETH We've just had another set-to.

DAVID What was it this time?

KENNETH I let out that I'm supposed to be meetin' a girl at the Imperial.

DAVID Oh 'eck!

KENNETH You can imagine what that started.

The two brothers exchange a resigned family look.

93

Stitching up the bully

BROOKSIDE

by Chris Webb and Julie Rutterford

Leo Johnson and Danny Simpson are mates at Brookside Comprehensive School. Danny is being bullied by Tinhead to do Tinhead's homework for him. These scenes are taken from three different episodes of 'Brookside'.

Characters

DAN SIMPSON

Danny Simpson (Dan or Daniel to his immediate family) is the sort of child who finds schoolwork a doddle. He has a huge appetite for learning and manages all his coursework with ease. Although at first he found it difficult to settle in Brookside Comprehensive (he had previously attended a private school), he has now settled in and found some friends... Dan has also had a few run-ins with Tinhead (the school bully) but he tends to fight back with his intellect rather than his fists.

LEO

Leo has a healthy respect for his dad, Mick – who, as a single parent, is very aware of his responsibility to his children. Leo generally gets on well with his sister, Gemma, although he sometimes considers her to be a pain when his dad tells him he has to look after her. Although he isn't a bad lad himself, Leo does occasionally get himself mixed up with the wrong crowd. For example, Tinhead, the school bully, once forced Leo to break into a neighbour's house and steal a computer with him. Leo was totally against the idea, but allowed himself to be pushed into doing it by his schoolmate.

TINHEAD

Tinhead (real name Timothy O'Leary) hates school. He also hates most of his schoolmates, especially the swots. However, this is not because he is stupid – in fact, he is rather a quick wit – it is more because he is lazy and doesn't want to work. He tends to operate in a group and uses the power of numbers to push his classmates around – he tends to pick on people he knows he can push around.

Sc. 1745.08 (EXT.) THE PARADE – DAY

Where DANNY *and* LEO *have exited the Trading Post and head towards the tunnel on their way back to school from their lunch break. Each has a can of Coke from which they drink as they talk. As* DANNY *swigs from the can then pulls a face.*

DANNY   I just cannot get rid of the taste of that cheese flan.

LEO   Always happens with late dinners ... you get the scraps ...

DANNY   (*Miffed*) Thanks to Hughsie, for keeping us back.

LEO   Did you do that Geography assignment that he's set us?

DANNY   I've done some of it ... I'll finish it off tonight.

LEO   (*Fed up*) I can't get me head 'round it. (*Grumbling*) I couldn't give a toss how many people moved to Liverpool 'cos of the Irish potato famine ... it's a waste of time learning that stuff.

DANNY Actually, I find demography[18] quite a fascinating subject.

LEO (*Misunderstanding*) Yeah, but I'm talking about Geography, Danny …

As they enter the tunnel we see TINHEAD *approaching them.*

DANNY (*Laughs*) I think if you read the question properly, you'll find we're on about the same thing.

LEO Can't you even get us some info off the Internet?

DANNY (*Grins*) I'm sure we could come to some sort of arrangement.

LEO *looks blankly as* TINHEAD *joins them.*

TINHEAD (*To* DANNY) 'Ey I wanna word with you, posh boy.

DANNY (*Appearing unperturbed*) I suppose you want that last lot of English homework … ?

TINHEAD Yeah and info on that Geography … you're supplying me now, remember?

LEO (*Chipping in*) I didn't even understand the title …

As they talk, DANNY *takes a large envelope from his bag.*

TINHEAD Yeah well … the ming's gonna save us from wasting our brain cell's on it.

DANNY (*A dig*) You'll have to save your last few, 'cos you're going to have to work sometime if you want a decent job when you leave school.

LEO (*Filling* DANNY *in*) He reckons he's joining the army.

TINHEAD (*He's a toughie*) Yeah, and soldiering's about using these … (*fists*) and this … (*Pretends to nut* DANNY) not about how many people died of some poxy disease hundreds of years ago.

[18] **demography** – the study of populations

DANNY (*Correcting him*) One hundred and fifty actually … (*Deliberately confusing him with words*) and I'd have thought using demography as a tool to chart the effects of changes in conditions within a community could prove useful for someone intending to spend his life in an extremely close-knit society such as the armed forces. (*Back to reality*) Besides, you need qualifications before the army will even look at you.

LEO (*To a dumfounded* TINHEAD) Danny's right. You know, you need qualifications for everything.

TINHEAD Just get the homework sorted, soft lad … And I want enough to sell on an' all. It's about time I made a bit of profit on this …

DANNY (*Staring hard at him*) Whatever you say …

As TINHEAD *snatches envelope from* DANNY *and waves it under his nose!*

TINHEAD (*Menacing*) You might think you're smart, don't ya'? But I'm gonna be the one coining it in. And I'll see you tomorrow, and make sure you've got it … all of it …

TINHEAD *laughs before swaggering off back to school.*

Sc. 1746.05 (EXT.) BROOKSIDE COMP. – DAY

Where it's breaktime and DANNY *and* LEO *stand together eating crisps and talking.* TINHEAD *over to them. He takes* DANNY*'s crisps, grabs a handful, stuffs them into his mouth, then hands bag back to* DANNY. *As* DANNY *goes to take the bag,* TINHEAD *lets it fall to the ground.*

LEO (*Cross*) Leave it, will yous.

TINHEAD (*Squaring up to* LEO) Or what, Johnno?

LEO *steps back scared.*

DANNY (*Diverting* TINHEAD) I suppose you're after the stuff on population changes in Liverpool?

TINHEAD (*Cocky*) If you're talking about the Geography homework for Hughsie, then yeah, I do.

TINHEAD *holds his hand out.* DANNY *takes a folder from his bag and extracts a set of papers, which he hands to* TINHEAD. *We see that there's a line graph illustration on the front.*

TINHEAD (*A threat*) This lot had better be worth an A …

We see LEO *peering over his shoulder looking at the homework.*

DANNY (*One last try*) It is … and it's worth paying for.

TINHEAD (*Laughs*) Want paying do you?

DANNY Yes I do.

TINHEAD (*Cocky*) Now why would I wanna do that when (*Snatches rest of work from* DANNY) some soft ming's giving it me free, and I've got a queue of customers waiting to buy it off me.

TINHEAD *stares hard at* DANNY *before sauntering away.* DANNY *stares after him and gives a little smile.*

Sc. 1746.08 (INT.) BROOKSIDE COMP. – DAY

LEO *and* DANNY *are walking along a corridor to their next lesson.* DANNY's *still holding the homework folder.*

LEO (*Handing him money*) Give us me homework, Danny … Hughsie wants it in now …

As LEO *reaches for the folder,* DANNY *pulls it away.*

DANNY You won't get far with that, Leo.

LEO *(Confused)* What d'you mean?

DANNY reaches in his bag and produces a large envelope. He takes two sets of papers out and hands one to LEO.

DANNY *(Smug)* Just a little something I prepared earlier …

As LEO looks at the work, we see it's very different to that which was given to TINHEAD. LEO takes the folder and compares the work.

LEO *(Confused)* Hold on a minute … that's not the stuff you gave Tinhead …

DANNY *(Taking back folder)* No … you and me have got something a bit different …

LEO You what?

DANNY *(Smirking)* What I gave Tinhead … it's a load of rubbish … I made it all up … as O'Leary's going to find out when Mr Hughes has had a chance to mark it.

LEO *(Nervous)* Are you soft or what? Tinhead's flogging this stuff to half the Geography group.

DANNY *(Tutting)* Then they're going to be wanting their money back, aren't they?

LEO *(Unhappy)* I hope you know what you're doing.

DANNY *(Smug)* 'Course I do, I'm not stupid …

LEO *(A warning)* He's gonna go ballistic, Danny …

DANNY *(Shrugs it off)* Let him … it'll be worth it … *(Relishing the thought)* just to get one over on that low life O'Leary …

As LEO looks extremely nervous, on DANNY confident he's got TINHEAD well and truly sorted.

Sc. 1749.02 (INT.) BROOKSIDE COMP./ CORRIDOR – DAY

LEO *and* DANNY *are walking along the corridor to their class when* TINHEAD *comes up behind them. He bangs* DANNY *on the head with a book.*

TINHEAD   (*To* DANNY) 'Ey toff ... I'll be expecting more of them essays next term, so unless you wanna lose your legs, you'll bring them in when I tell you, right?

DANNY   (*As they walk along, to* LEO, *as though* TINHEAD *isn't there but said for his benefit*) Did you know that we only use a seventh of our brain? (*Said for* TINHEAD'*s benefit*) Mind you, some people are only born with a seventh of their brain ...

TINHEAD   (*Turns, clenching his fist in* DANNY'*s face*) Do you want this rammed down your throat?

DANNY   (*Playing it cool, moving* TINHEAD'*s fist away*) No thanks ... I don't know where it's been.

TINHEAD   (*To* DANNY) You're asking for a good hiding you lad.

He shoves DANNY *into the wall as* LEO *looks worried.* TINHEAD *moves away down the corridor.*

LEO   (*To* DANNY, *of* TINHEAD) Aren't you even bothered about what he's gonna do to you when he finds out you've stitched him up?

DANNY   (*Putting on a convincing brave front*) No ... I can handle him.

But LEO *is convinced* DANNY *is heading for trouble.*

Sc. 1749.08 (INT.) BROOKSIDE COMP. – DAY

LEO *and* DANNY *are walking along the corridor.*

DANNY (*Satisfied grin on his face*) Not bad, 'ey, Leo? The only two in the class with top marks.

LEO (*Chuffed*) I can't believe it …

DANNY (*Smug grin*) It was worth it just to see the look on Tinhead's face. What do you reckon he'll get? A week's detention, suspended …

LEO All's I know is if I were you, I'd keep me head down for a bit. He'll be out to get you … and so will all the others you've stitched up …

They turn the corner into another corridor where we see TINHEAD *and the rest of the class lined up outside the Head's Office.*

LEO (*To* DANNY) Er, d'you think we'd best walk the other way.

DANNY (*Revelling in this*) What? And miss all the fun?

LEO *reluctantly follows* DANNY *down the corridor. As they near the Head's Office, all eyes turn on them … including* TINHEAD, *who sees red.*

As DANNY *walks past with* LEO, *unable to look at any of his classmates in the face, he glances over at* TINHEAD, *a smug grin on his face. This is too much for* TINHEAD, *who leaps up and pins* DANNY *against the wall.*

DANNY (*Trying not to look ruffled; to* TINHEAD) Temper, temper.

TINHEAD (*White with anger; to* DANNY) You're dead. (*To* LEO, *who is about to try and slope off*) And you.

DANNY (*Of* LEO; *to* TINHEAD, *who still has him pinned against the wall*) Oh no, Leo can't take any credit … it was all down to me.

TINHEAD I couldn't give a toss who did it – you're both gonna get it.

> TINHEAD *is about to throttle him when a teacher walks past, giving* DANNY *the chance to slip away.*

DANNY (*Still refusing to be ruffled; to* TINHEAD) I'd love to stay and chat, but I've got things to do.

TINHEAD (*As* DANNY *walks off; points at him*) Dead!

LEO Let's go.

> LEO *and* DANNY *carry on walking down the corridor … will they escape from* TINHEAD?

Films

1895   The first film show by the Lumiere brothers in Paris.

1896   The Lumiere brothers show their films in Britain.

Within 30 years, an enormous, worldwide, silent film industry developed.

1929   Release of the first 'talking picture', *The Jazz Singer*.

In the late 1940s, 20 million people went to the cinema every week. By 1995, it was about two million.

In spite of this potted history of cinema-going, film has a great attraction still, even though much viewing of it may now be on television, with its relatively small and poor-quality picture, via broadcast or video. At its best it has the ability to move, delight, inform and surprise us like the best in any medium.

'Reading' film can be very difficult when there is just so much happening on the screen and soundtrack. As a result some people are better readers of film than others; they are simply more aware of all that is going on. But you can learn to improve your own reading, by training yourself to concentrate on all the different elements at once. Otherwise, you may be missing half the fun.

The selections here are taken from two famous works: an outstandingly popular American adventure film (*Raiders of the Lost Ark*) and a classic British thriller (*The Third Man*).

Raiders of the Lost Ark

Screenplay by Lawrence Kasdan
Story by George Lucas and Philip Kaufman

FADE IN:

EXT. PERU – HIGH JUNGLE – DAY

*Mountain peaks against sky in dense, lush rain forests filled
with the varied SOUNDS OF THE JUNGLE. Ragged,
jutting canyon walls are half-hidden by the thick mists.
A group of men makes its way along a narrow trail across
the green face of the canyon.*

At the head of the party is an American, INDIANA JONES. *He
wears a short leather jacket, a flapped holster, and a
brimmed felt hat; there is a whip swinging at his hip. Behind
him come some* QUECHUA INDIANS. *They act as porters and
are wrangling the two heavily-packed donkeys. Bringing up
the rear are two Spanish Peruvians,* SATIPO *and* BARRANCA.
BARRANCA *speaks to the Indians in Quechua.*

*An Indian chops at a branch and is faced with a horrific
stone sculpture of a Chachapoyan demon. The Indian
screams and runs away as birds fly out from the
undergrowth.* INDIANA JONES (INDY) *steps forward quickly
and gazes at the sculpture as more birds fly out.* SATIPO *and*
BARRANCA *exchange looks, then glance over their shoulders as
they move on.*

INDY *leads* SATIPO *and* BARRANCA *along a stream towards
heavy mist. Visibility is cut to about five feet.*

As INDY *jumps the stream, he sees a short dart sticking from a tree. He extracts it, fingering its point, then drops it and moves on.* BARRANCA *and* SATIPO *run forward and* SATIPO *picks up the dart. He tastes his finger and spits.*

SATIPO

The Hovitos are near. The poison is still
fresh. Three days. They're following us.

BARRANCA

If they knew we were here, they would
have killed us already.

INDY *walks through shafts of light in thick forest and* SATIPO *and* BARRANCA *follow.*

SUBTITLE FADES IN: 'SOUTH AMERICA – 1936.'

Standing in front of a waterfall, INDY *pulls out a torn, aged piece of parchment, then takes a second piece from* SATIPO *and fits them together.*

BARRANCA *quietly draws his pistol and raises it towards* INDY.

INDY*'s next move is amazing, graceful and fast. His right hand slides up under the back of his leather jacket and emerges grasping the handle of a neatly-curled bullwhip. With the same fluid move that brings* INDY*'s body around to face the Peruvian,* INDY *uncoils the whip to its full, ten-foot length. It flashes out to knock the gun from* BARRANCA*'s hand to the ground, where it goes off.* BARRANCA *runs away while* SATIPO *watches, shocked and frightened.*

INDY *steps forward from the shadows and we see his face for the first time. He gathers the whip, then walks up a hill to the face of the vegetation-enshrouded Temple of the Chachapoyan Warriors, 2000 years old. He quickly ducks inside, then reappears as* SATIPO *catches up, carrying a back pack.*

INDY *pulls a bag from the pack and bends down, starting to fill it with sand.*

INDY
This is it. This is where Forrestal cashed in.

SATIPO
A friend of yours?

INDY
A competitor.

INDY *tucks the bag of sand into the waist of his pants.*

INDY
He was good … He was very, very good.

SATIPO
Se-or, nobody's come out of there alive!
Please …?

INDY *turns* SATIPO *around, pulls a small shovel from the pack, and throws the pack to the ground.*

INT. TEMPLE – INCLINED PASSAGE – DAY

INDY *and* SATIPO, *who carries a torch, walk up the slightly inclined, tubular passage from the main entrance. The interior is wet and dark, hanging with plant life and stalactites. Their echoing footsteps intermittently overpower the sounds of loud dripping, whistling air drafts, and scampering claws.* INDY *wipes away thick spiderwebs with his whip.*

As INDY *steps out of a shadow, three huge black tarantulas are crawling up the back of his jacket. He doesn't notice them and disappears into another shadow. When he emerges,* SATIPO *sees the tarantulas and stops, terrified.*

SATIPO

(*Hoarsely*)   Se-or!

INDY *looks at him, sees what he's pointing at, and casually brushes off all three spiders with his rolled whip, as he would a fly.* SATIPO *sees one on his own shoulder and, unable to speak, works his jaw silently.* SATIPO *pirouettes slowly – his back is covered with tarantulas. They crawl over his chest, neck and back.* INDY *flicks them to the ground and they scuttle away.*

The men reach an arch in the hall. The small chamber ahead, which interrupts the hall, is brightly-lit by a shaft of sunlight from high above. INDY *pauses, gesturing with his whip.*

INDY

Stop! Stay out of the light.

He ducks under the light shaft; then, out of the way, raises his hand into the light. Giant spikes spring together from the sides of the chamber with a ferocious CLANG! Impaled on the spikes are the remains of a white man, half-fleshed, half-skeleton, in explorer-type garb. The body trembles gently on the spikes.

SATIPO *screams in terror as* INDY *stares thoughtfully at the corpse.*

INDY

(*Softly to himself*)   Forrestal …

INDY*'s whip flashes, curling around a beam, and he jumps across an endless pit. He throws the handle of the whip to* SATIPO, *who swings forward. The beam begins to sag and* INDY *quickly reaches forward to grab* SATIPO*'s belt and pull him up.*

INDY
Hurry up!

SATIPO *scrabbles against the edge of the pit as rocks begin to fall, then lunges forward, grabbing* INDY. INDY *wedges the whip handle into the wall and leaves it strung to the beam.*

They round the corner to the sanctuary, passing a huge brass sun. The sanctuary is a large domed room with a stone floor in an intricate design. INDY *and* SATIPO *look across the wide room at the altar. There, in the supreme hallowed spot, in the middle of the room, is a tiny gold figurine,* INDY*'s real objective.*

SATIPO
Let us hurry! There is nothing to fear here!

He starts forward and INDY *grabs him and holds him back.*

INDY
(*Softly*) That's what scares me.

He releases SATIPO, *and with an unlit wooden torch, squats and taps a stone tile. The tile sinks, and from a carved mask in the wall a tiny arrow shoots, slamming into the torch.*

INDY *nods, stands and looks around the sanctuary. The entire room is honeycombed with the masks.* SATIPO *sees this too, and is properly impressed.* INDY *points at* SATIPO.

INDY
Stay here!

SATIPO
If you insist, se-or.

INDY *begins his careful walk across the sanctuary. Stepping only on the centre tiles in the complicated pattern, he almost appears to be doing a martial arts kata. He begins to lose his balance and* SATIPO, *who has been sitting across the wall, rises.*

SATIPO

Ssss …

INDY *recovers his balance and reaches the altar. The tiny idol looks both fierce and beautiful. It rests on a pedestal of stone.* INDY *looks the whole set-up over very carefully as he takes the small, canvas drawstring bag from his waist. Concentrating, he bounces it a couple of times in his palm, then pours some of the sand out. It's clear he wants to replace the idol with the bag as smoothly as possible.*

SATIPO *watches, wide-eyed, as* INDY *suddenly makes the switch! The idol is now in his hands, the bag on the pedestal. He turns to* SATIPO, *grinning, and starts to step off the altar. Then the pedestal beneath the bag drops several inches. This sets off an aural chain reaction of steadily increasing volume as some huge mysterious mechanism rumbles into action deep in the temple.*

The sanctuary begins to rumble and shake. As INDY *follows the fleeing* SATIPO, *rocks smash onto the sanctuary floor and arrows shoot from the mouths of the masks.*

SATIPO *swings over the black pit, making it just as the whip comes undone, leaving* INDY *without an escape.*

INDY

Give me the whip!

SATIPO

Throw me the idol!

Behind SATIPO *a slab of rock begins to lower, blocking the exit.*

SATIPO

No time to argue! Throw me the idol,
I throw you the whip!

INDY *tosses the idol to* SATIPO, *who drops the whip on the floor.*

INDY

(*Yells*)   Give me the whip!

SATIPO *runs under the dropping slab of rock.*

SATIPO

Adios, se-or.

INDY *runs in a full stride to the edge of the pit and jumps into space. He doesn't make it. His body hits the far side of the pit and he begins to slide out of view. Only wild clawing with his fingers at the edge of the pit stops his descent. With just the tips of his fingers over the edge, he begins pulling himself up, grasping at a vine. The vine loosens and* INDY *slides lower, then scrambles out. He grabs his whip and slides under the slab just before it closes.*

As he looks up, he sees SATIPO, *impaled on the spikes where they had found Forrestal. His eyes are wide, blood running from the wounds in his forehead and chest.* INDY *grabs the idol, which has fallen to the ground.*

INDY

Adios, stupido.

INDY *shoots out of a cut-off hallway and turns towards the exit. The rumbling is very loud and now we see why: right behind* INDY *a huge boulder comes roaring around a corner of the passage, perfectly form-fitted to the passageway. It obliterates everything before it, sending the stalactites shooting ahead like missiles.* INDY *dashes for the light of the exit through a haze of cobwebs. He dives out the end of the passage as the boulder slams to a perfect fit at the entrance, sealing the temple.*

EXT. TEMPLE & JUNGLE – DAY

INDY *lies on the ground, gasping for air. A shadow falls across him and he looks up. Looming above him are three* HOVITOS WARRIORS *in full battle paint and loincloths. They carry spears. As* INDY *looks down a line of more warriors, he sees* BARRANCA. *The* HOVITO *behind* BARRANCA *pushes him forward and he falls. He has many arrows in his back.*

We see a pair of legs step over BARRANCA*'s body. As* INDY *looks up:*

BELLOQ
Doctor Jones …

BELLOQ *is a tall, impressive white man, dressed in full safari outfit including pith helmet. His face is thin, powerful; his eyes, hypnotic; his smile, charming yet lethal. His French-accented speech is deep, mellifluous, wonderful.*

BELLOQ
… again we see that there is nothing
you can possess which I cannot take
away. And you thought I'd given up.

INDY *starts to pull his gun from its holster and the* HOVITOS *move forward, their weapons ready. He hands the gun to* BELLOQ.

BELLOQ
You chose the wrong friends. This time
it will cost you.

INDY
(*Eyeing the Hovitos*)   Too bad, the Hovitos … don't
know you the way I do, Belloq.

INDY *produces the idol and hands it to* BELLOQ.

BELLOQ

(*Speaks in Hovitos; then*)   Yes, too bad. You could
warn them … if only you spoke Hovitos.

With that, BELLOQ *turns dramatically and holds the idol
aloft for all the* HOVITOS *to see. He speaks to them in Hovitos.
There is a murmur of recognition and all the* INDIANS,
*including Belloq's escorts, prostrate themselves on the ground,
heads down.*

INDY *is immediately up and running towards the edge of the
clearing. The* HOVITOS *lift their heads and* BELLOQ *motions
them after* INDY. *He stands aside, holding the idol, and
laughs.*

EXT. THE JUNGLE – INDY'S RUN – DAY

INDY *runs like hell, past the stone demon, onto steadily
falling terrain. And always, close behind, there is a swift
gang of angry* HOVITOS.

*Occasionally, they get close enough to send a dart or spear
whizzing past* INDY's *head.*

EXT. THE RIVER – DAY

*An amphibious plane sits in the water beneath a green cliff.
Sitting on the pontoon and fishing is* JOCK, *the British pilot.
He rises as he hooks something.*

INDY *runs up the hill pursued by the* HOVITOS.

INDY

(*Yells*)   Jock! Start the engines! Get it up!

JOCK *looks up, holding his fishing pole, looks back at the pole.*

INDY

Jock! The engines! Start the engines! Jock!

The HOVITOS *shout as* JOCK *drops the pole, hops in, and fires up the plane's engines.* INDY *reaches a spot on the cliff above the plane, grabs a vine, and swings into the river. He comes up, swims to the plane, and grabs a pontoon as the* HOVITOS *shout and shoot arrows at the plane.* INDY *climbs up into the cockpit and the plane lifts off from the water.*

EXT. PLANE – AIRBORNE – DAY

As the plane lifts off, INDY *jumps in his seat.*

INT. COCKPIT – DAY

A huge boa constrictor is crawling on INDY*'s lap.*

EXT. PLANE – AIRBORNE – DAY

INDY *reacts, pointing down into cockpit.*

INDY
There's a big snake in the plane, Jock!

JOCK
Oh, that's just my pet snake, Reggie.

INDY *shudders.*

INDY
I hate snakes, Jock! I hate 'em!

JOCK
Come on! Show a little backbone, will ya?

EXT. JUNGLE – DUSK

The plane soars off over the dark jungle.

The Third Man

Script by Graham Greene

Main characters

ROLLO (HOLLY) MARTINS

A Canadian, aged about 35. He has been invited to
Vienna by his old friend, Harry Lime, to write
propaganda for a volunteer medical unit Lime runs.
A simple man who likes his drink and his girl, with
more courage than discretion. He has a great sense of
loyalty towards Lime, whom he first met at school, and
even his blunderings are conditioned by his loyalty.

His love for Anna arises from the fact that she shares
his devotion to Lime. Unlike Lime, he has never made
much out of life. He is an unsuccessful writer of
Westerns, who has never seen a cowboy, and he has no
illusions about his own writing.

HARRY LIME

Harry Lime has always found it possible to use his
devoted friend. A light, amusing, ruthless character,
he has always been able to find superficial excuses for
his own behaviour. With wit and courage and
immense geniality, he has inspired devotion both in
Rollo Martins and the girl Anna, but he has never felt
affection for anybody but himself. He has run his
medical unit to help his racket in diluted medicine.

ANNA SCHMIDT

An Estonian, and therefore officially a Russian citizen, she has been living in Vienna and working as a small-part actress under the protection of forged Austrian papers procured for her by Harry Lime, whom she loves. Unlike Martins, she has few illusions about Harry.

COLONEL CALLOWAY

In charge of the British Military Police in Vienna. A man with a background of Scotland Yard training: steady, patient and determined in his work – a man who is always kindly up to the point when it interferes with the job, who never gets angry (because it would be unprofessional) and regards Martins with amused tolerance.

SERGEANT PAINE

An ex-London policeman whose spiritual home is in the Tottenham Court Road and the streets around it.

Context

Post-war Vienna was 'divided into four zones, each occupied by a power – the Americans, the British, the Russians and the French. But the centre of the city – that's international, policed by an International Patrol.' It is the period of the Black Market when racketeers would 'run anything, if people wanted it enough and had the money to pay'. Lime's racket of watering down penicillin, to make more money out of selling it, has resulted in people dying or becoming brain-damaged. When Martins gets to Vienna, he is told that Lime has been run down by a car and buried.

Scenes 86–98

86 THE ORIENTAL. LOCATION (NIGHT)
An International Police car drives up and the patrol enters
through a door marked: 'Out of Bounds to Allied Personnel'.

87 THE ORIENTAL: BAR AND DANCE FLOOR
(NIGHT)
The patrol enters. It is a dreary, smoky little night club. The
same semi-nude photographs on the stairs, the same
half-drunk Americans at the bar, the same bad wine and
extraordinary gins – you might be in any third-rate night
haunt in any other shabby capital of a shabby Europe. A
waiter is handing out a large pile of notes to MARTINS. *The*
cabaret is on and the International Patrol wait and take a
look at the scene. The Americans at the bar never stir, and
nobody interferes with them. The cabaret comes to an end.
MARTINS *rises. One of the dance girls, who has been watching*
the waiter give him the notes, comes up and speaks to him.

DANCE GIRL

It's early, dear.

MARTINS

What? What did you say?

DANCE GIRL

(*Puzzled*)   It's early.

MARTINS *looks at her as if he does not understand a word*
and goes to the stairs. Then he comes back to the GIRL, *who is*
watching him.

MARTINS

Did you ever know a fellow called Harry Lime?

DANCE GIRL

No. Did you?

MARTINS *shakes his head, less as if he were saying no than getting something out of his hair. Dissolve.*

88 EMPTY CLUB (NIGHT)
The seats are being piled up and a waiter and a girl are quietly pushing MARTINS *out.*

89 ANNA'S STREET (NIGHT)
MARTINS *is walking unsteadily in the street. The rain is dripping from gutters, but he has not bothered to put on a coat.*

90 ANNA'S LANDING (NIGHT)
MARTINS *knocks on the door and* ANNA *opens it. She is in a dressing-gown.*

ANNA

What is it? What's happened to you?

MARTINS

I've found out everything.

ANNA

Come in. You don't want to wake the house.

91 ANNA'S ROOM (NIGHT)

ANNA

Now, what is it? I thought you were going to keep away. Are the police after you?

MARTINS

I don't know.

ANNA

You're drunk, aren't you?

MARTINS

(*Sulkily*)   A bit.
(*Angrily*)   I'm sorry.

ANNA

Why? Wish I had a drink.

MARTINS

I've been with Calloway. Learnt everything. We were
both wrong.

ANNA

You'd better tell me.

*She sits down on the bed and he begins to tell her, swaying
slightly with his back to the window.*

MARTINS

You know what penicillin does.

ANNA

Not really.

MARTINS

It's supposed to cure people of things. They've been
stealing penicillin here, mixing it with water, I don't
know what. People have been dying from it – wounded people, children. I suppose they were all in it –
Kurtz, Tyler – even that doctor.

*He goes to the window, and turns again to her. Over his
shoulder we look down into the dark street.*

92 ANNA'S STREET. LOCATION (NIGHT)

*Somebody looks up at the lighted window. The shadow of a
bombed building falls across his face so that we cannot see it.
He walks towards a door and stands in the shadow – we
cannot see him – a cat walks across from the other side of the
road in his direction – it is mewing.*

93 DOORWAY. LOCATION (NIGHT)

The cat comes to the man's legs purring and rubs itself
around the bottom of his trouser-leg – it is hungry.

94 ANNA'S ROOM (NIGHT)

MARTINS

I'm not a doctor: I don't understand it all, except
Harry made seventy pounds a tube – he ran the
business.

ANNA *looks away from the laughing, cheery photograph of*
HARRY.

ANNA

You were sober when they told you? They really
proved it?

MARTINS

Yes. So you see, that was Harry.

ANNA

(*Putting her hand over her eyes*)
He's better dead. I thought perhaps he was
mixed up ... but not with that.

MARTINS

(*Getting up and walking about*)
For twenty years – I knew him – the drinks he liked,
the girls he liked. We laughed at the same things.
He couldn't bear the colour green. But it wasn't true.
He never existed, we dreamed him. Was he laughing
at fools like us all the time?

ANNA

(*Sadly*) He liked to laugh.

MARTINS

(*Bitterly*)   Seventy pounds a tube. And he asked me to write about his great medical charity. I suppose he wanted a Press Agent. Maybe I could have raised the price to eighty pounds.

ANNA

There are so many things you don't know about a person you love, good things, bad things.

MARTINS

But to cash in like that ...

ANNA

(*Angrily*)   For heavens sake, stop making him in your image. Harry was real. He wasn't just your friend and my lover. He was Harry.

MARTINS

Don't talk wisdom to me. You make it sound as if his manners were occasionally bad ... I don't know ... I'm just a bad writer who drinks too much and falls in love with girls ... lots of girls ... you.

ANNA

Me?

MARTINS

Don't be such a fool – you know I love you?

ANNA

If you'd rung me up and asked me, were you dark or fair or had a moustache, I wouldn't have known.

MARTINS

Can't you get him out of your head?

ANNA

No.

MARTINS

I'm leaving Vienna. I don't care if Kurtz killed Harry
or Tyler – or the third man. Whoever killed him, it
was justice. Maybe I'd have killed him myself.

ANNA

A man doesn't alter because you find out more.

MARTINS

I hate the way you talk. I've got a splitting
headache, and you talk and talk ... You make me
cross.

Suddenly ANNA *laughs.*

ANNA

You come here at three in the morning – a stranger –
and say you love me. Then you get angry and pick a
quarrel. What do you expect me to do?

MARTINS

I haven't seen you laugh before. Do it again. I like it.

ANNA

(*Staring through him*)
There isn't enough for two laughs.

MARTINS *takes her by the shoulder and shakes her gently.*

MARTINS

I'd make comic faces all day long. I'd stand on my
head and grin at you between my legs. I'd learn a lot
of jokes from the books on After Dinner Speaking ...
I'd ...

ANNA *stares at him without speaking.*

MARTINS

(*Hopelessly*)   You still love Harry, don't you?

ANNA

(*Picking up the copy of her play*)
I've got to learn my lines.

ANNA *looks through the pages of her script and back to* MARTINS. MARTINS *drops his hands. As he goes towards the door, he turns and makes half an apology, half an accusation.*

MARTINS

You told me to find a girl.

95 ANNA'S STREET. LOCATION (NIGHT)

MARTINS *walks rapidly away. Passing along the street, he becomes aware of a figure in a doorway on the opposite side of the street. The whole figure is in darkness except for the points of the shoes.* MARTINS *stops and stares and the silent motionless figure in the dark street stares back at him.* MARTINS' *nerves are on edge. Is this one of* CALLOWAY'*s men, or* TYLER'*s, or the Austrian police?*

MARTINS

(*Sharply*)   Do you want anything?

No reply. MARTINS *takes a few steps on and then turns again.*

Have you been following me? Who's your boss?
(*Still no reply.* MARTINS *is irascible with drink. He calls out sharply.*)

Can't you answer?

A window curtain opposite is drawn back and a sleepy voice shouts angrily to him.

WOMAN

Seien Sie ruhig. Gehen Sie weiter. (Be quiet. Go away.)

The light shines across straight on the other man's face.

MARTINS

Harry!

MARTINS, *in his amazement, hesitates on the edge of the pavement. The woman has slammed down the window and the figure is again in darkness, except for the shoecaps. Then it begins to emerge, but before* MARTINS *has a chance of seeing the face again, an International Police car approaches down the street. The figure steps back, and as the car comes between them, the figure makes off in the dark. By the time the car has passed, there is no sign of the stranger – only the sound of footsteps.* MARTINS *pursues, but the sound dies out. He passes a kiosk and comes out into a fairly well-lighted square which is completely empty. He stands around in bewilderment, unable to decide whether he was drunk or whether he had seen a ghost, or indeed* HARRY. *Dissolve.*

96 KIOSK SQUARE. LOCATION (NIGHT)

CALLOWAY *stands looking at the square with* MARTINS *and* PAINE.

MARTINS

You don't believe me …

CALLOWAY

No.

MARTINS

It ran up here and vanished.

They stare at the empty moonlit square. PAINE *and* CALLOWAY *exchange glances.*

CALLOWAY

Where were you when you saw it first?

MARTINS

Down there – fifty yards away.

CALLOWAY *turns his back on the square and looks down the street past the kiosk.*

CALLOWAY

Which side of the road?

MARTINS

This one. And there aren't any side turnings.

They begin to walk down the street.

CALLOWAY

Doorways …

MARTINS

But I could hear it running ahead of me.

They reach the kiosk.

CALLOWAY

And it vanished with a puff of smoke, I suppose, a clap of …

He breaks off as his eye lights on the kiosk, and he walks across to it, pulls open the door. We see the little curling staircase going down.

It wasn't the German gin, Paine.

CALLOWAY *leads the way down, shining a torch ahead.*

97 THE SEWERS. LOCATION (NIGHT)

A strange world unknown to most of us lies under our feet: a cavernous land of waterfalls and rushing rivers, where tides

ebb and flow as in the world above. The main sewer, half as wide as the Thames, rushes by under a huge arch, fed by

*tributary streams: these streams have fallen in waterfalls
from higher levels and have been purified in their falls, so
that only in these side channels is the air foul. The main
stream smells sweet and fresh with a faint tang of ozone, and
everywhere in the darkness is the sound of falling and
rushing water.*

MARTINS

What is it?

*CALLOWAY without replying moves ahead, across a bridge
which spans a waterfall.*

PAINE

It's only the main sewer, sir. Smells sweet, don't it?
They used it as an air-raid shelter in the war, just like
our old tube.

They come up with CALLOWAY who is leaning over the bridge.

CALLOWAY

I've been a fool. We should have dug deeper than a
grave.

98 CENTRAL CEMETERY. LOCATION (DAWN)

*A small group make their way down an avenue of graves. At
the end of the avenue three men are engaged in digging. The
group consists of CALLOWAY, a BRITISH JUNIOR OFFICER,
MARTINS, an Austrian POLICE OFFICER, and an OFFICIAL
from the City Council, who carries an umbrella. The group
pass the graves of Beethoven, Schubert and Brahms, and
CALLOWAY pauses just long enough for us to take in their
inscriptions. As they approach Lime's grave, thin rain begins
to fall, and the Austrian OFFICIAL opens his umbrella and
offers to share it with CALLOWAY. One of the men comes over
to CALLOWAY and speaks in German.*

MAN

Wir sind jetzt am Sarg. (We've reached the coffin.)

CALLOWAY *and the* OFFICIAL, *still under the same umbrella,*
go up to the graveside and stand looking down. The OFFICIAL
moves round the side of the grave to examine the body from
another angle. He turns across the grave to CALLOWAY *and*
shrugs his shoulders. CALLOWAY *takes one look and moves*
away, passing MARTINS. *He nods to* MARTINS *to take a look.*
MARTINS *reluctantly does so, then quietly joins* CALLOWAY *as*
they walk away.

OFFICIAL

Did you know him, Colonel?

CALLOWAY

Yes. Joseph Harbin, medical orderly at the 43rd
General Hospital.
(*To* JUNIOR OFFICER)
Next time we'll have a foolproof coffin.

Study activities

*Activities marked with an asterisk are more involved activities which could be developed into coursework or substantial work for folders.

NEWSPAPERS AND MAGAZINES

Anorexic models

1 Reporters are taught to ask six questions: the five 'W's – Who? What? Where? When? Why? – and How? Write out the information relating to each of the six in the first piece – the news item.

2 Read the three pieces of writing. Then write a letter to the editor of *Vogue*, supporting or criticising her use of very thin models.

3 Hotseating. Appoint one member of the group as editor of *Vogue* and another as Mr Rees. Question them both about their attitudes to the use of skinny models in magazines.

4 *Write out five key phrases from Mr Rees's statement. Show them to five classmates and write down whether they agree with him or not. Try to get reasons for people's opinions plus any other stories or evidence they have. Then write up the results as a project report.

World Press Photos of the Year

1 These photos were chosen as best 'news' photos of their years. First, look at the photos only. Choose the one which affects you most strongly. Write out a detailed description of all you can see in the picture, including people, places and things. Mention what you think the photographer wanted you to focus on and how that relates to the rest of the picture in terms of size, shape and position. What ideas and feelings do you get from looking at the picture?

2 Now read the caption which the World Press put alongside the photo. What additional understanding do you get? Does this make the emotional impact of the image stronger for you or not?

3 Look through some newspapers and magazines to find photos of positive situations – things being praised or celebrated. Describe one of these in the same detail as above.

Comparisons

4 Compare the photos in a tabloid and a broadsheet newspaper for the same day, with regard to number, subject-matter, size and impact.

5 *Take contrasting photos of your school or area. Make half of them positive images, so that it appears an attractive place; make the other half negative. Think of the structure and style as well as the subject-matter. Then write an illustrated account of your work, explaining what you hoped the images would show.

"It was the Christians"

1 Describe the effect on you of reading this news item. What thoughts and emotions does it make you feel? Which people does Robert Fisk want us to:

a) admire
b) condemn
c) pity?

Give examples of Robert Fisk's skilful use of language to show his feelings.

2 Write brief answers to the six basic questions – Who? What? Where? When? Why? How? – about these events. Then, with examples, describe the crucial differences in style and purpose between this summary and the way Robert Fisk has described the events.

3 *Write a news item for an Israeli or Christian militia newspaper, reporting the events at Chatila. Then write about how the item shows the attitudes you have found in Robert Fisk's piece.

4 Prepare a talk to your class: should detailed portrayals of violence on television be restricted to real-life examples?

Oasis: No split

1 Look again at the front page of the *Daily Mirror* for 13 September 1996. Note down the following:

a) the number of news items covered;
b) the main headlines;
c) what each picture shows.

2 With a friend or in a group, talk about the front page. Would it make you buy the newspaper?

3 *Imagine you are Oasis's agent or manager. Write your diary entry for the day of the 'confrontation'.

4 *Design the front cover of a tabloid newspaper. Write the headlines, chose the stories and pictures. Then write an account of the effect you have tried for.

5 *Look closely at the front page of a national or local newspaper. Make notes on the seven points below:

   a) layout and presentation, such as how much space is devoted to particular items
   b) any interesting ways of presenting the page
   c) choice of stories and headlines
   d) use of pictures
   e) who will read it
   f) the overall impact you think the editor was aiming for and how successful you think the front page is.

(You may find it useful to look at an inside page, to help you work out why the above ingredients were on the front page.)

Use these notes to write an account of what you think the editor was trying to achieve.

And you thought twisters only hit America

1 Read the whole piece carefully. Write out:

a) any phrases that indicate it was written for a popular tabloid;

b) five things you learned from the article.

2 In a similar style to 'T for Terror', make a one-to-ten list for 'R for Rain' or 'S for Sunshine'.

3 *Write a short radio documentary to cover the main points and experiences described in the article. Include sound effects and music as well as commentary and dialogue. Then make a tape of the programme. Finally, compare how the techniques of each medium – newspaper article and radio documentary – have been used to put across information.

Web of Fear!

1 Write out the stages that Adelaide Dugdale went through in overcoming her phobia, starting:

a) Absolutely terrified of spiders.

2 Roleplay one of the Friendly Spider sessions. Read through the piece carefully and allocate roles for the organisers and for members of a group showing different levels of fear of spiders.

3 Design an advert for the Friendly Spider Programme at London Zoo, using information from the article.

4 *Do you (or someone you know) have a phobia? Write a magazine article about how it has affected you (or them) on a particular occasion, and say how it might be helped. Then add your own comments on the article, explaining how your purpose, style and sense of who is going to read it have affected the way you have written.

Journo-lists

1 A lot of newspapers and magazines include games or trivia – like these lists. Make ten jokey points about a subject of your choice or one of the following:

a) Ten embarrassing things that parents do
b) Ten things to avoid in wedding photos
c) Ten imaginary television programmes that nobody would watch.

ADVERTISING AND PUBLICITY

Folio of ads: 1884–1996

Three health drinks: Horlicks, Lamplough's Pyretic Saline and Lucozade

1 a) Make a list of all the illnesses, diseases and conditions that the drinks claim to cure or help.

b) Who do the three ads seem to be aimed at?

c) In what ways do the companies try to persuade people to buy their drinks? Which approach most appeals to you?

d) What human needs do the advertisers try to connect with their products? How convinced are you by them?

2 Make a screenplay based on the Horlicks cartoon strip. Scene One has been done as a model:

You want the moon, darling?

Scene One

Exterior. Night. River Thames Embankment.

PHILIP VERNEY, *a playwright, is with his fiancee,* JOAN.

PHILIP   … and in a week we'll be married, Joan. Fletcher loves the play…the new one'll be even better – and – you want the moon, darling?

---

3 *Try to create an ad for a health drink which would appeal to all ages. You can put it in the form of a poster or film or play script. Then write about how your presentation tries to widen its appeal.

Comparisons

4 What differences and similarities are there in the way that the two drinks, Lucozade and Horlicks, are presented in two different media. Think in terms of stories, characters, language and visuals.

Social and historical contexts

5 What clues are there in these ads about when they were created and what society was like then? Look at references to people, places, things, medicine, language and behaviour, as well as the style of the ad. Make notes on each and then write up your findings.

Two modern ads: Benetton and S-Curl

6 Write a detailed description of one of these ads, including characters, mood, gestures, clothing, setting, lighting and composition. How is the product presented? How effective is the ad?

7 Write a serious or jokey story which shows success or happiness being linked with the use of one of these products.

8 *Make an ad for one of these two products structured and presented in the style used for one of the health drinks. Write in detail about what you have done.

Comparisons

9 List and write about the main differences in style and structure you can see between the advertisement for Lamplough's and any one of the modern ads. Think about the presentation, the kind of visuals and words used, the space given to each and the general approach.

Amnesty International leaflet

Amnesty International is a charity which fights against abuses of human rights.

1 Discuss with a partner or in a group:
   a) what kinds of abuses are given here;
   b) whether Amnesty should use these shocking examples;
   c) why you think Amnesty used the letter format;
   d) how you feel about this request for funds.

Make notes and then report your conclusions to the class.

2 Write a letter to the Director of Amnesty, giving your opinion of:

a) the leaflet's content, style and overall tone;

b) the advantages and disadvantages of using a letter format to raise money.

Bradwell leaflet

1 What are mentioned as the main attractions of the Bradwell nature trail? To whom might they appeal?

2 Nuclear power stations have not always received good publicity. Why did Magnox choose to develop this project and produce this leaflet? Do you think it will help Bradwell's image?

3 *Make a public relations leaflet for visitors to your school. It should be no larger than two A5 sides. What pieces of information will you write down to create the best possible impression? Note any illustrations you want to include.

Then describe how you've used the following to achieve your aims:

a) common questions about the school

b) choice of contents

c) the style of writing and illustration

d) structure

e) layout and presentation.

RADIO

Jane Eyre by Charlotte Brontë

1 Discuss with a partner or in a group: which scene in the play do you think would be the most effective on radio? Why?

2 Write down your impression of Jane's character in the radio play. Take into account what she says and does, how others behave towards her and what they say to her and about her.

3 Make your own tape-recording of the script. Remember that you only have sounds to create feelings and thoughts in your audience. Think about appropriate use of voices (accent, tone, pitch, speed, etc.), natural sounds (wind, creaking doors, etc.) and music.

Comparisons

4 *This extract from the dramatisation for radio by Michelene Wandor covers most of the first 30 pages of the novel.

Here is the opening of the novel *Jane Eyre*:

> There was no possibility of taking a walk that day. We had been wandering, indeed, in the leafless shrubbery an hour in the morning; but since dinner (Mrs Reed, when there was no company, dined early) the cold winter wind had brought with it clouds so sombre, and a rain so penetrating, that further exercise was now out of the question.
>
> I was glad of it; I never liked long walks, especially on chilly afternoons: dreadful to me was the coming home in the

raw twilight, with nipped fingers and toes, and a heart saddened by the chidings of Bessie, the nurse, and humbled by the consciousness of my physical inferiority to Eliza, John, and Georgiana Reed.

With a partner make notes on any similarities and differences between these paragraphs and the start of the play. Then write a comparison of the openings, including comment on the two media.

Hancock's Half Hour:
Sunday Afternoon at Home

1 Copy out any of the following words which apply to Hancock and then add an example from the script to prove it: mature, childish, creative, unimaginative, sarcastic, patient, short-tempered, small-minded, generous, fussy, relaxed, sincere, hypocritical.

2 Although this kind of programme is known as situation comedy, the characters are as important as the situations. Write brief descriptions of the characters of Bill, Sid and Hattie, including your impressions of age, appearance, clothes, mannerisms etc.

3 Alan Simpson, one of the scriptwriters, said about this programme: 'It was very risky using so much dead time, which was … absolutely taboo in a light entertainment show'.

a) What is this 'dead time' and how is it shown in the script?

b) Why is it risky on radio?

c) Describe a couple of moments when 'dead time' is used well.

4 Like a number of radio programmes, *Hancock's Half Hour* was translated into television. In the latter you saw the setting, which you had to imagine on radio. Describe and sketch the room they are in at Hancock's famous address: 23 Railway Cuttings, East Cheam.

5 *Continue this radio script, bringing in other things to make the time pass, but none of them successful. You could include some from the original script, such as knitting, watching the telly, gossiping about neighbours, playing records, and doing impressions.

Word of Mouth: Manhattan Transfer

1 Snapping is a game played among friends in America. Write a paragraph explaining the game, its uses and how it developed.

2 Tell the dramatic story of how 'Two Brothers and a White Guy' got together? What is unusual about their act?

3 Discuss: would this programme have been better on television?

4 Monteria explains that the jibes are not at real people; it is just a game where the cleverest sentence wins. With a partner, make up some clever 'snaps'. Then perform the act for your class.

5 *Listen to a radio programme. It can be one that you listen to regularly or it could be a new programme – a play or documentary, for example. (If possible, record the programme, so that you can listen to it in more detail afterwards.) As you listen, jot down notes on when radio works well and where it is limited in what it can do.

6 *Write an extended review of either the radio programme you listened to for 5 or the 'Word of Mouth' broadcast. Include in your review accounts of the following and their success:

a) the subject-matter and storylines
b) the use of different characters and voices
c) the overall style and atmosphere
d) memorable sequences (e.g. creating an atmosphere or sense of place)
e) any use of striking devices, such as contrasts or parallels, special effects, silence or music
f) your assessment of the whole programme.

TELEVISION

Monty Python's Flying Circus: The Dead Parrot

1 *Monty Python* is full of surreal comedy: the kind of thing that happens in dreams, when funny peculiar becomes funny ha-ha.

a) Make a list of six peculiar things in this sketch.
b) Describe the part you find most comical and say why you do.

2 Write a review of the sketch for

a) a tabloid newspaper (30 words maximum);
b) a broadsheet newspaper (100–150 words).

Indicate what the sketch is about, describe its style and say what you thought of it. You may not need as much as

30 words for the tabloid piece; for example: 'Dead parrot – dead crazy – dead laugh'.

3 *Write your own *Monty Python* style sketch. Either bring a fictional character into an everyday, real-life situation (like Superman turning up in your school) or put a living person into a fictional world you know well from books, television or films.

Absolutely Fabulous: Fashion

1 a) A lot of the humour in this scene comes from the reversal of roles of the two characters. Divide your page into two columns: one headed 'Saffron'; the other, 'Edina'. In the columns write lists of opposites to describe them (e.g. Saffron – mature; Edina – childish).

b) Most of the humour is in the dialogue and would work on radio but some would not. Explain why three examples of humour would not work on the radio.

2 a) Write the diary entry for Edina or Saffron for this start to her day.

b) Imagine you are to direct an actress as Edina or Saffron. Write notes, in script order, on how (volume, pace, tone of voice etc.) she might speak particular lines and what kinds of gestures and movements she might make and when.

3 What would Edina and Hancock (pages 46–55) think of each other? Choose either one and write down their thoughts about the other.

Comparisons

4 *Write about differences in the kind of character, event, language and humour in *Absolutely Fabulous* and *Monty Python's Flying Circus*.

Jimmy's

1 How does this documentary try to get our interest at the start? Think about the types of illness and stages of treatment; the range of people mentioned; the language of the voice-over.

2 Which of the people involved came across strongly? Choose (a) a patient and (b) one of the medical staff. Write a short character description of each, using some of their words as evidence.

3 Some of the dialogue is technical; the shots of operations are gory; yet *Jimmy's* is very popular. Explain its appeal, using examples from this episode.

4 *A documentary is to be made about your school. Write
a) a list of sequences you would like to film for it;
b) an opening voice-over, designed to hook the viewer;
c) an explanation and justification for your choices and opening.

Casualty: Value For Money

1 a) From the first scene alone, what would you expect this episode of *Casualty* to focus on? Are these expectations followed through?

b) Write a summary of each scene in one or two sentences. Then describe any patterns you can see in the way the drama is put together.

2 What are the main differences between regular characters and the others, in terms of dialogue, action and how they are introduced?

Comparisons

3 What are the main similarities and differences between this drama and the extract from *Jimmy's* on pages 71–6? Think about the kinds of storyline, settings, characters, dialogue and structure.

Coronation Street: The Barlows

1 Discuss: what in the script tells you that this is the first episode?

2 Drama is often seen as a situation involving conflict or opposition. Make a list of all the conflicts and opposites in character, speech and situation you can find in this scene.

3 Write a review of this scene, describing the characters, situation and what happens. Say whether you would continue to watch it.

4 *a) Write a new scene for *Coronation Street*: breakfast at the Barlows' house the next morning.

b) Explain what knowledge you have used from the original scene.

Social and historical contexts

5 This extract from *Coronation Street* was written in 1960. From the descriptions of characters, the dialogue and what happened, write about any differences between society in 1960 and now.

Brookside: Stitching up the bully

These scenes follow one storyline but they are taken from three different episodes of *Brookside* – numbers 1745, 1746 and 1749. So, scenes involving other characters are not included.

1 What seems to be the relationship between Danny and Leo? Explain your answer by describing what they say and do?

2 *Brookside* has been praised for being realistic (based on real life).

a) Describe three things about these scenes which are realistic.

b) Real life cannot always be included in soaps. Think of three real-life topics which would not be included in a soap. Explain why.

3 Write a short review of these *Brookside* scenes for a magazine – say which one! – concentrating on the storyline, characters and dialogue.

4 *The scriptwriter wrote at the end of Scene 1749.08: 'Will they escape from Tinhead?' Try to answer the question by writing the *Brookside* scene when Tinhead next meets up with Danny and Leo.

5 a) The critic David Aaronovitch has divided characters from the soap genre into types: 'There must be a matriarch (mother figure); when they appear in the text I mark them "M". There will usually be adulterers (A), harmless idiots (HI), entrepreneurs (E), troubled teenagers (TT), bad guys (BG), violent boyfriends (VB), Winona Ryder lookalikes (WR), melting hunks (MH) and get-ahead girls (GG).' Write out David Aaronovitch's abbreviations and one soap character that fits each description. Add any abbreviations you can think of for other types of characters you often get in soaps.

b) Describe a scene from a soap you have watched, using as many of the abbreviations as possible.

Comparisons

6 *Compare how young men and women are shown in any popular television programme. Think about:
a) individual characters: their appearance, clothing, possessions, speech, habits and behaviour;
b) general characteristics: any qualities a number of characters share;
c) any unusual characters;
d) any thoughts you have about the way young men and women are presented.

7 Compare how young men are shown in the extracts from *Coronation Street* and *Brookside*.

FILM

Raiders of the Lost Ark

1 Describe the incidents in the script which could make you jump if you were a viewer of the film. Which of these reactions would be the result of visuals, which of sound effects and which of both?

2 a) Write out the main elements of Indy's character? Think of what he says, what he does and how others behave towards him. How does the author want us to see him? What do you think of him?

b) In many American films, Mexicans and South Americans are stereotyped as cowardly and untrustworthy. Write about the way the characters of Satipo and Barranca are represented.

3 *Raiders of the Lost Ark* is an example of a popular genre – the adventure film. Audiences expect certain kinds of character, action, style, etc. in such a film.

a) Describe the features of the genre that appear in this script.

b) Which of the features of adventure films do you like/dislike?

4 *Think about the genre in a completely different way. Script a new adventure for Indy and Satipo, with them behaving in very different ways: Satipo doing all the heroic deeds and Indy relying on him. Write about all the changes you have made to the genre of the adventure film.

5 *a) Read carefully the opening paragraphs of the scene set inside the temple – from their entry up to where the tarantulas 'scuttle away'. Write this sequence as a detailed script. (Use different sizes of shot, camera movements and unusual angles.)

> Shot sizes and camera movements to consider: close-up (CU), mid-shot (MS), long shot (LS), wide shot (WS), pan to left (pan L) or right (pan R), zoom in (ZI) or out (ZO), tilt up (TU) or down (TD), tracking shots (horizontal or vertical).

b) Describe how you have tried to bring out the action and mood.

The Third Man

These scenes are taken from the classic British thriller *The Third Man*, written by the celebrated author Graham Greene.

1 Write down the number of each scene (86–98) in turn and after each write a one-sentence summary of its content.

2 Describe the flow of Anna's feelings and thoughts in Scenes 90–94.

3 *a) Make a storyboard for Scene 95. Draw a series of rectangles (6cm x 3cm) and then sketch in them what you would see in each shot. Think about shot size and angle. Underneath each rectangle describe any camera movements and what sounds you would hear.

b) Explain what you have chosen to put in close-up and why.

Social and historical contexts

4 Note down what evidence there is in the script of *The Third Man* about when it was written and what society was like then. Make notes on people, places, things, attitudes, behaviour and language.

Comparisons

5 Compare this extract with that from *Raiders of the Lost Ark*. Both films are set in foreign countries earlier this century.

a) What are the main differences in terms of characters, settings, actions, and dialogue? Make a list for each of the above for both films and note the differences.

b) If you were a film director, which of the two films would you prefer to make? Explain why you have made your choice.

6 *Although every film is different, it has things in common with some others. It belongs to a genre: thriller, musical, period drama, western, comedy, science fiction, etc.

Look carefully at a feature film and make notes on what evidence there is for it belonging to a particular genre. Make notes on:

a) the storyline
b) characters: appearance, dress, language, attitudes, behaviour, etc.
c) settings
d) music and sound effects
e) any unexpected elements.

Then write an account of the film, showing how it does and does not live up to what an audience expects of the particular genre. Where possible, compare the film with others you know.

Addison Wesley Longman Limited
Edinburgh Gate, Harlow
Essex CM20 2JE, England
and Associated Companies throughout the World.

This educational edition first published 1997
Second impression 1998

Editorial material set in 10/12.5 pt Stone Sans
Printed in Singapore through Addison Wesley Longman China Limited

ISBN 0 582 28932 7

The Publisher's policy is to use paper manufactured from
sustainable forests.

Acknowledgements

We are grateful to the following for permission to reproduce photographs
and other copyright material:

The Advertising Archive, page 26; Amnesty International, pages 28–31;
Colorific!/David Turnley/Black Star, page 6 above; Luster Products,
page 27; Magnox Electric plc, pages 32–4; Magnum Photos/James
Nachtwey, page 6 below; Mirror Syndication International, page 12; Rex
Features, page 4; SmithKline Beecham Nutritional Healthcare, page 22.

We are grateful to the following for permission to reproduce copyright material:

Amnesty International for a letter by Abas Faiz and a text extract from their pamphlet entitled *Torturers, Rapists, Murderers* (1996); the writer Janice Bhend for her letter to the Editor 'Hungry and in Vogue' in The *Guardian* 1.6 96; BBC Rights Archive/Simon Elmes on behalf of Russell Davies for post-production script of programme 1 'Manhattan transfer' from *Word of Mouth* Series 8, transmitted 20.8.96. Presenter: Russell Davies, Producer Simon Elmes; BBC Worldwide Ltd./the authors' agent for an extract from the script of 'Sunday Afternoon at Home' by Ray Galton and Alan Simpson from *Hancock's Half Hour: The Classic Years 1987*; BBC Worldwide Publishing/the author's agent for an extract from the script 'Fashion' by Jennifer Saunders from *Absolutely Fabulous* (1993); Brookside Productions Ltd./Phil Redmond, Creator and Executive Producer of *Brookside* for extracts from 'Character descriptions and scripts in episodes/scenes: 1745/08, 1746/05, 1746/08, 1749/02 and 1749/08'; EMAP for an extract from the article 'Web of Fear' by Adelaide Dugdale from *Bliss* Magazine, June, 1996, pages 64–6; Express Newspapers Ltd. for article 'Ad chief gives Vogue a lean time' by Annie Leask from *Daily Express* 31.5.96, page 4; Granada Television Ltd. for an extract from script of Episode 1 of *Coronation Street* by Tony Warren; Lucasfilm Ltd. for an extract from script of *Raiders of The Lost Ark* by George Lucas and Philip Kaufman, screen play by Lawrence Kasden (1995) TM & © 1981 Lucasfilm Ltd. All Rights Reserved. Courtesy of Lucasfilm Ltd.; Mirror Group Newspapers for article 'OASIS: No Split' by Matthew Wright from *Daily Mirror* 13.9.96, page 1; Nuclear Electric plc for an extract from pamphlet for Bradwell Nature Trail; Random House UK Ltd. for an extract from script of 'The Dead Parrot' sketch by Chapman, Cleese, Gilliam, Idle, Jones and Palin from *Monty Python's Flying Circus*, VOL 1, published by Mandarin Books 1990; Smith Kline Beecham Consumer Health Care for TV advertisement script for 'Lucozade Sport' by Ogilvy and Mather Ltd.; the author, Allan Swift, for an extract from the script 'Value for Money', *Casualty*, Series 8, Episode 18 – Granada TV; Ewan Macnaughton Ltd. on behalf of Telegraph Newspapers for Editorial 'Let there be Flesh' from *Daily Telegraph* 1.6.96; Times Newspapers Ltd. for extract from article 'It was the Christians: The Massacre at Chatila', 16–17 September, 1982 by Robert Fisk from *The Times* 20.9.82. ©Times Newspapers Ltd. 1982; UGC UK Ltd. for an extract from script *The Third Man* by Graham Greene; the author, Micheline Wandor, for an extract from the script of episode 1 *Jane Eyre* by Charlotte Bronte, dramatised for radio by Micheline Wandor; Yorkshire Television for an extract from the post-production script transcribed from a Yorkshire TV Video of *Jimmy's*, series 12, programme 5 (No PNF255/18).

We have been unable to trace the copyright holder of the article 'Twisters' by Derek Elsom and would appreciate any information which would enable us to do so.